Dinner is Ready!

A complete guide to freezing
30 meals in just one day!

By Deanna Buxton

Red
Timer
Inc.

Cover art by Ryan Lindahl

Library of Congress Control Number: 2006939214

ISBN: 978-0-9787765-0-3

Enjoy all 30 Meals in One Day™ titles by Deanna Buxton:
Dinner is Ready
Lunch is Ready
On the Side

For additional books, software, and other products, visit us online at
www.dinnerisready.com
www.30MealsinOneDay.com

A double batch of love, appreciation and my deepest gratitude to my beautiful family for enduring the seemingly endless testing of recipes. To my adorable children, Erin (who's favorite dinner was a tasty but very mushy spaghetti recipe that did not make the cut), Scott (by who's taste I can tell if something is *really* good), Alanna (who is a joy to cook for since she likes anything I make) and Samuel (who loves me always and would never tell me if he didn't like it anyway). To my one-in-a-million husband, David, who is not only the love of my life but also my editor, without whom this book would be nothing more than a jumble of words on paper.

For Beth,
who believed in me

Contents

Introduction 1

Chapter 1   Why Freeze? 3

Chapter 2   What is Freezer-Worthy? 5

Chapter 3   Things That Will Make Your Life Easier . . .9

Chapter 4   Choosing Recipes 17

Chapter 5   Lists That Will Make Your Life Easier 23

Chapter 6   The Day Before 29

Chapter 7   Cooking Day 33

Chapter 8   Packaging for the Freezer 39

Chapter 9   The Freezer 45

Chapter 10   Thawing 49

Chapter 11   Sample Order of Events 51

Chapter 12   Other Options 57

Chapter 13   Blessing the Lives of Others 61

Chapter 14   Shortcuts 63

Chapter 15   Recipe Section

        Slow Cooker 70

        Oven .100

        StoveTop 118

        Assemble 155

        Recipe Index 229

Introduction

Do you love to cook but have days that you don't have time to cook? Perhaps you hate to cook, but don't you still *have* to cook?

Are you frustrated because no matter how efficiently you manage meetings, carpools, lessons, practices and home-work, you still have to find time to make dinner? Have you noticed that no matter how bountiful the meal you place before your family for dinner, they will want dinner again tomorrow?

Have you noticed that no matter how great a mother you are for going to countless baseball games, dance recitals and trips to the pool, as soon as the trip is over, they are hungry and you suddenly feel like a lousy mom because it is time for dinner and there is no dinner? There is no dinner because you have been busy being the good mother in the baseball stands!

You now have three basic solutions. 1. Stop for fast food, again, which only works occasionally. 2. Feed them macaroni and cheese or something less desirable. 3. Prepare a lovely dinner only to find out that now no one is hungry because while you were cooking, they managed to find last year's Easter candy.

Of course, you could keep your freezer stocked with prepack-aged, frozen foods from the freezer section of the grocery store. They will cost you a bundle and you never know which ones you will like and which ones you will suffer through until they are gone, but they truly are convenient. Then again, you could create your own convenience. You could stock your freezer with meals that *you* have prepared. You will save money and know that your family likes what you place before them.

Whatever keeps you busy, whether it be family, career, busy lifestyle, or you simply don't like to cook, suffer no more. With *Dinner is Ready* as your guide, you can spend just one day cooking and fill your freezer with 30 dinners. No matter how busy your day has been, dinner can be ready, hot and delicious in minutes.

Every aspect of the process is covered in this book. Everything from the equipment that will make your life easier to over 150 freezer-worthy recipes to choose from. Chapter 11 is a sample outline with complete, step-by-step instructions to prepare 30 meals in one day. The recipes are listed and the order of events is outlined for you. Each recipe is delicious, family friendly and fairly simple. Following this example will guide you through a positive first experience. Each subsequent experience will be easier as you develop your own style and shortcuts.

This process will be helpful to you regardless of the number of people you are cooking for, since recipes are packaged in meal-size portions, whether for one, two or any family size. You may not have time, ability or desire to prepare 30 meals in one day. Be sure to consider the other options outlined in chapter 12. These options will provide you with freedom and convenience, and save you money.

No matter what your circumstances, having 30 meals in your freezer makes it possible for you to say "dinner is ready," and that is a beautiful thing!

Chapter 1

Why Freeze?

Why freeze? Because you are busy! Your time is valuable. Some days you don't get home in time to prepare dinner. Some days, even though you are home, you still do not have time to cook. Some days you have time but perhaps you are tired or you just don't feel like cooking. Freeze to create your own convenience.

You can purchase plenty of convenience at the grocery store. Take a stroll down the freezer isle of your favorite grocery store. Notice the wide variety of frozen foods that can be purchased. Maybe your family will like them, maybe they won't. Maybe the meals you find are healthy, and maybe they are not. Maybe you can afford them, maybe you cannot. How many times have you purchased a frozen food, only to find out that it contains an ingredient that your family does not like, there is not enough filling, it is too dry, or it simply does not taste good? When you freeze it yourself, you have the advantage of freezing only those things your family enjoys, the way your family prefers them. And you know exactly *what* your family is eating. No more mysteries! Freeze what they like, what is good for them and what you can afford.

You can save time and money as well as create freedom for yourself by cooking one day and ending up with meals ready for many days. Having a selection of meals in the freezer gives you the freedom to be gone all the way up to mealtime and still place a delicious dinner before your family. You can enjoy what you are doing and stop worrying about what your family is having for dinner.

Daily convenience is important. So is the freedom you can create for yourself when you are entertaining guests. Wouldn't you rather spend time with your guests than spend time slaving away in the kitchen preparing food for the masses? If you know in advance that guests are coming, whether it be for the evening, overnight or for an extended stay, you can prepare the meals, freeze them and spend the time you save with your guests! You can even prepare family-plus-guest-sized meals for those times that you have unexpected guests at dinner time.

Dinners in your freezer will not completely eliminate the time you need to spend in the kitchen each day, but it will certainly shorten it. How many times have you come home and thought that a particular food would be great for dinner but you don't have the time to make it from scratch? If you have dinners in the freezer, in some cases you can have the main dish on the table in about the same time it takes to prepare the salad and bread. 30 dinners in your freezer, prepared in only one day, is a beautiful thing!

Just because you have 30 dinners in the freezer does not mean that you *must* eat only meals from the freezer for the next 30 days. There will be days you eat elsewhere - maybe at a friend's house, at grandma's house, at a restaurant, or at the spaghetti dinner fund raiser at school. The rest of the time, you can be prepared at dinner time no matter how demanding your day.

There may be days that the stars line up and you have time to cook - and feel like cooking dinner! These are the days that perhaps you could prepare a recipe that does not make the freezer-worthy list.

Chapter 2

What is Freezer-Worthy?

A recipe is considered freezer-worthy if it can be prepared, frozen, thawed, heated and served, and still be delicious and appealing to those who consume it. A general rule is that, if you see it frozen at the store you can probably freeze it successfully at home. However, some things do not freeze well.

Fresh, raw potatoes do not freeze well in any recipe. They will turn black and ugly. Cooked potatoes usually turn mushy and watery after being frozen. You can, however, cook potatoes in some recipes. Cubed potatoes in some soup type recipes are usually good, especially in a recipe in which the potatoes are intended to be cooked until they start to disintegrate, such as chowder.

Mashed potatoes can sometimes be frozen. Recipes with a topping of mashed potatoes can usually be successfully frozen. Single servings of mashed potatoes covered with recipes, such as **Cream Cheese Chicken** on page 86, are also usually good. Make the mashed potatoes very thick and test freeze a small portion before freezing an entire recipe.

Most recipes that call for boxed dehydrated potatoes, such as **Scalloped Pork Chops** on page 223, can be frozen. The potatoes absorb moisture during freezing, thawing and baking, and soften up nicely.

While freezing potatoes can be fussy, you can sometimes side step the potato issue by substituting commercially frozen potatoes in a recipe. Frozen potatoes, such as hash browns, from the store have been commercially processed with machinery that removes excess moisture. This freeze-dry vacuum-processing is not possible for home freezing so only use purchased frozen potatoes. In some recipes, such as **Cheesy Ham and Potatoes** on page 217, the frozen potatoes can be added without thawing them first.

If you are unsure of freezing potatoes in a particular recipe, freeze only a small portion. In a few days, heat it and taste it to see if it makes your "freezer-worthy" list.

The freezing process softens vegetables. Vegetables have a high moisture content and when this moisture freezes it expands and breaks the rigid cell walls, causing the vegetables to lose their crunch. In most cases this is not even noticed since cooking softens vegetables anyway. However, if you are preparing a stir-fry recipe and you prefer your vegetables slightly crunchy, you should not freeze them. You may prefer to prepare everything except the vegetables and freeze. On the day you serve the meal, you can add the fresh vegetables.

Fresh, raw vegetables, except for onions and peppers, need to be cooked briefly, or blanched, prior to freezing. For example, if you are freezing an Assemble recipe, such as **Chicken and Rice** on page 204, which calls for fresh sliced carrots, the carrots will need to be cooked briefly. Cooking them for about 2 minutes in boiling water is usually sufficient before adding them to the rice and freezing the meal. If you use previously frozen vegetables in your recipes no further cooking is required before freezing. In most Assemble recipes there is no need to thaw the vegetables first.

Add toppings such as buttered crumbs and French fried onions at baking time. They absorb moisture from the meal and can get soggy in the freezer. Top with shredded cheese at the end of baking time. Cheese can be frozen if it is shredded first. If you freeze a block of cheese and then try to shred it, it will crumble.

Pasta can be frozen successfully but it should be undercooked. On the back of most pasta packages the recommended cooking time is listed. When you are cooking pasta to be frozen in a recipe, cook the pasta for two minutes less than the shortest recommended cooking time. For example, if you are cooking bow tie pasta and the instructions on the package suggest that you cook it for 9 to 11 minutes, cook it for only 7 minutes. Only add the pasta AFTER the water is boiling and set your timer as soon as you drop the pasta into the boiling water. You may think that the pasta could not possibly be done enough to add to your recipe, however, the pasta will continue to absorb moisture during the entire process of freezing, thawing and then heating. If you start with pasta that is fully cooked, there is the possibility that it will get mushy. A timer becomes all the more important since overcooking the pasta can be disastrous and you won't even know it until you serve the meal later.

If you find that you do not like the texture of pasta that has been frozen, even when it is undercooked before freezing, you may want to prepare the recipe and exclude the pasta. On the day you serve the meal, cook the pasta and add it to the meal.

An exception to this method of cooking pasta is lasagna. You don't need to cook your lasagna noodles at all! And you don't need to buy the expensive "no boil" kind, either. Any lasagna noodle is just fine. The lasagna will be layered with sauce and cheeses. By the time you assemble the lasagna, freeze it, thaw it and then bake it, the noodles will have absorbed enough liquid to make perfect lasagna. You will find that your lasagna will hold its shape on the plate. No more sliding lasagna! Manicotti can successfully be made using uncooked manicotti tubes as well. They are also much easier to fill when uncooked.

Instant rice turns mushy and disintegrates. Deep fried foods lose their crispness. The crispness can be at least partially regained by placing it under the broiler in your oven or toaster oven for a minute or two.

Some cooking sources tell you not to freeze dairy-based sauces, gravies and soups. While it is true that frozen dairy-based recipes are ugly and can even separate and turn lumpy when thawed, this is not a reason to not freeze them. Heat is a true miracle! When heated and stirred, most sauces, gravies and soups return to their smooth creamy texture. Sometimes the recipes thicken a bit and you may need to stir in a little milk, broth or water. Heat and stir, and they usually blend right back to a beautiful consistency.

The test for "freezer-worthiness" is, *"Do you like it after it has been frozen?"* After it is frozen, thawed and heated, can you tell that it has been frozen? If you can tell it has been frozen, you don't want it on your freezer-worthy list. You are not freezing leftovers! What makes leftovers taste like leftovers? Leftovers can taste dried out, thick and overcooked. Freezing is a marvelous method for food preservation. When frozen properly, the food you serve your family will taste as delicious as if made that day! The intention is to freeze food at or before its peak so you are always serving fresh tasting food. Fully cooked meals such as Slow Cooker, StoveTop and Oven recipes should be frozen as soon as cool enough to go into the freezer. Assemble recipes should be frozen as soon as preparation and packaging is complete.

Chapter 3

Things That Will Make Your Life Easier

There is some basic equipment you should have in order to prepare many recipes in one day. The items listed in this chapter will make your life easier on Cooking Day. Most of these things you probably already have in your kitchen. For each item that you do not have, carefully consider its value and consider adding it to your collection.

Two Sets of Measuring Cups

Two sets of measuring cups are essential. More specifically two *different* sets of measuring cups. One set for dry ingredients, one set for wet ingredients. If you only use one set of measuring cups, how much time will you waste washing out wet ingredients and then drying the measuring cup so you can measure something dry, only to have to measure something wet again? A set of measuring cups for wet ingredients and a separate set for dry ingredients is invaluable.

A *set* of "wet" measuring cups could include a set of nesting measuring cups with 1 cup, 1/2 cup, 1/3 cup and 1/4 cup measures, and a 2-cup glass liquid measure. A true liquid measure is one that when filled to capacity leaves room to move the cup without spilling the contents. Use this type to measure large quantities of liquid, such as water or chicken broth. This type of measure requires that you check the amount at eye level. Since there is certain amount of guessing involved to determine where "level" is, especially when measuring 1 cup or less, a set of nesting measuring cups is particularly helpful, even though they are not true liquid measures. When measuring ingredients of 1 cup or less, hold the measure over the bowl or very near to it, fill it to the brim and pour it in. There is no need to wash out the measuring cups unless flavors will collide, and even then usually a quick rinse is all it will need. There is no need to dry it out since a speck of water probably won't hurt *any* recipe you are preparing for dinner.

A *set* of "dry" measuring cups could be a different shape or color of nesting measuring cups. If you purchase plastic measuring cups be sure to get the kind that the measurement numbers (1/4 cup, 1/3 cup, 1/2 cup, etc.) are in raised plastic. If they are just painted on, eventually the paint will come off and you will be left guessing which is the 1/4 cup and which is the 1/3 cup.

Use whatever combination of metal, plastic and/or glass measures that you are comfortable with. Just be sure you have a set for wet and a set for dry.

Two Sets of Measuring Spoons

You will need two different sets of measuring spoons for exactly the same reason you need two different sets of measuring cups. One set for wet, one set for dry. Keep things consistent and use the same type of measuring spoons and measuring cups to measure your dry ingredients and the same type of measuring spoons and measuring cups to measure your liquid or wet ingredients. In other words, if you use your metal set of measuring cups for wet ingredients, also use a metal set of measuring spoons for measuring liquid. If you choose plastic cups to measure dry ingredients, use plastic measuring spoons to measure dry. As with the plastic measuring cups, if you purchase plastic measuring spoons, be sure the measurement number is in raised plastic, not stamped or painted on.

You might also consider getting a cute little glass measure for measuring up to 2 tablespoons at a time. It looks just like the larger 2 cup version in miniature. It has markings for 1 to 6 teaspoons, 1/2 to 2 tablespoons and 1/4 to 1 ounce measurements. It truly comes in handy when making double or triple recipes. This handy little item can be found at specialty kitchen stores and sometimes in the kitchen gadget section of grocery stores.

Canning Funnel
A canning funnel has a big opening at the bottom of the funnel. It is used for filling narrow mouth canning jars. The bowl of the funnel fits into a quart freezer bag. A serving spoon fits right through the mouth of the funnel. This makes for a marvelously easy, neat and tidy way to fill pint or quart freezer bags. Using a canning funnel ensures that you will not drip anything on the zipper part of the freezer bag while filling it. It is maddening to drip sauce on the zipper part of the bag then have to clean it off without spilling the contents and making a bigger mess. Save yourself the hassle and the cleanup time and get a canning funnel. You can usually get one anywhere you find canning supplies.

Large Mixing Bowls
Depending on your family size, you may be making double or even triple recipes. If this is the case, large mixing bowls come in really handy. Three or four is a good number. If you have several bowls, you can make several things at nearly the same time. Popcorn bowls are inexpensive, fairly easy to find and make perfect large mixing bowls.

Large Mixing Spoons
You will need some fairly large spoons to mix your double batches. If the largest spoon in your drawer is the one you use to serve the peas, be kind to yourself and get some large spoons. However, for some cold recipes, especially meatloaf and meatball recipes, consider using your hands. It is faster, easier and more thorough than using a spoon.

Large Pans

Making double or triple recipes of chili, spaghetti sauce, soup, etc. requires large pans. You can use your canner or any large capacity pan.

Disposable Foil Baking Pans

When you make chicken enchiladas, lasagna, or other layered dinners you will not want to put them into your baking dishes and lose your dish to the freezer for a month or longer. You probably do not have as many pans and baking dishes as you want to make dinners either. Instead, layer the dinners right into disposable foil baking pans. These nifty, can't- do-without-'em items come in every size, from very small to really large and every size in between. Small loaf pans make perfect lasagna for one or two. Small cake pans are perfect for small families. You can get 8 x 8-inch square, 9-inch round, 9 x 13-inch, and even larger. Choose the size that will be meal-size for your family.

They make for very easy cleanup, and are inexpensive enough to simply throw away. They can be reused if you wish, if you wash them out carefully. You can get these pans at most grocery stores. If not, ask the manager if they *can* get them for you. Most dollar stores and chain super stores carry them, too.

Extra Heavy Foil

You will need to cover the foil pans before you put them into the freezer. Use **Extra Heavy** foil. You will find it in the same place you get regular foil. It is much wider and heavier than regular foil. Read the box carefully before you buy it. There is *heavy duty* foil that is slightly heavier than regular foil but it is *not* freezer foil. Be sure to get Extra Heavy Foil. It will usually say *for freezing* somewhere on the box, usually on the back. It is the heaviest foil available to protect your food from freezer burn. Cut the foil about 1-inch larger than the pan and crimp this excess under the edges of the pan. There is no need to wrap the entire pan. Be careful with this stuff. The edges are stiff and very sharp.

Kitchen Scissors

A pair of kitchen scissors is a real time saver. Trimming or cutting up chicken, raw or cooked, is so much easier with scissors. Using scissors to cut some vegetables, such as green onions, makes the task easier. Cutting up bacon is a breeze with scissors. Seems you can never get that last strand of bacon with a knife! You can cut a groove in the cutting board and still have that one skinny piece left! Use scissors! You will also need to cut your freezer foil to size depending on the size of the pan you are covering. Don't worry. Cutting foil is actually beneficial to the scissors. The foil helps sharpen your kitchen scissors as you cut.

Non-stick Cooking Spray

You may have many pans to grease. Spraying each pan with non-stick cooking spray will eliminate the time consuming and messy job of greasing each pan with shortening. It saves on calories, too.

Freezer Bags

Most dinners that you will put into the freezer can be stored in freezer bags. Good quality zipper freezer bags are won-derful. You can fill, press out the air, label, and layer them tidily in your freezer until you want them. Choose the size you need according to the size of your family and the size of the dinners you will be freezing. When filling a gallon bag, fold down the top few inches. This will protect the zipper from getting anything on it. It will also make the bag stable enough to stand up on its own, making it easier to fill. Use a canning funnel to fill quart or pint-sized bags.

Disposable Plastic Storage Containers

These invaluable little beauties are wonderful. They come in many sizes and can be put in the freezer. You may want to put your spaghetti sauce, soups, etc. in them. These are especially perfect for freezing single servings. Choose the ones that are easily re-usable, and are dishwasher, freezer and especially *microwave safe*.

Permanent Marker

Before each meal finds its way to the freezer, it will need to be labeled. Any medium point black permanent marker will do. If you use any other type of marker and it gets wet, you will be wondering what you are having for dinner. A lot of markers refuse to mark on some surfaces, such as masking tape or anything slick. Each dinner should be labeled with the name and the cooking instructions. You are busy! You don't have time to be looking up the cooking instructions when you want to serve a meal from your freezer. Write down everything you will need to know in order to serve the meal. Include the oven temperature, baking time, topping with crumbs or cheese, etc. You can either write directly on the bag, box or foil, or you can attach a label to each.

There is now a *30 Meals in One Day* computer program available. The *Dinner is Ready* version contains every recipe in this book and allows you to enter any other recipes you desire. This program will adjust recipe sizes and print recipe cards. It will generate printable grocery shopping lists. It will print your chosen Menu complete with the date and the number of each meal you have frozen. It will print labels, ready to put on meals for the freezer, complete with recipe title and cooking/serving instructions. This program will streamline your efforts and is available in stores and at **www.dinnerisready.com**.

Timers

Even if you never use a timer, you will want to get one or more. Your stove probably has one. Your microwave probably has one, too. If they don't, get one or more of the hand held kind. Having at least one additional timer makes it possible to time two things at the same time. You will need to time your pasta since it is imperative that it be undercooked. Even if you have a really reliable "internal clock," when cooking several things at the same time, you will find that it becomes increasingly more difficult to keep track of when each is done. Having multiple timers relieves your internal clock, eliminates the guess work and helps prevent overcooking.

Food Processor

When it comes to chopping onions, anything that can make the task easier and quicker is a necessity. Use a food processor for uniform pieces of chopped onion. It also makes chopping bell peppers and other vegetables a breeze. You can chop or mince onions, mushrooms and even chicken in a fraction of the time that it would take to do the same job with a knife and cutting board. If your processor has a grating attachment you will love how easy it is to shred cheese, too.

Rice Cooker

A rice cooker is certainly not a necessity, until you use one once. With a rice cooker you can cook a lot of rice to perfection every time. Turn it on, it times itself, turns off when the rice is done and you can dip into it each time you need rice. Clean up is a breeze. A rice cooker is certainly a beautiful thing!

Slow Cooker

A slow cooker is a marvelous cooking method that produces some of the yummiest of dinners with very little effort. A slow cooker provides even heat yet you don't have to watch it or stir it or ever worry about anything sticking or burning. Keep one or two working throughout the entire cooking day. Consider starting one working the night before cooking day, as well. Having one slow cooker is wonderful and, if you want to cook more than two slow cooker recipes in a day, having two slow cookers is a beautiful thing!

Multiple Trash Containers

Having many trash cans all around the kitchen will definitely make your life easier. In the course of making 15 recipes, how many things will you throw away? If you have to walk to the kitchen sink, open the cupboard door and lean over to toss away trash under the sink each time you throw something away, you will definitely waste a fair amount of time and effort. Place trash cans throughout your kitchen, not in your way, but wherever you will need them so that you don't have to take more than a step or two to toss anything away.

You don't need to purchase additional trash cans nor do you need to take trash cans from your bathrooms! Your trash cans do not have to be actual trash cans. Brown paper bags work perfectly. Brown paper grocery bags are not too big and in the way, yet big enough to hold a fair amount. Easily attainable, too. When the bagger at the grocery store asks you "paper or plastic," just say "paper!"

Chapter 4

Choosing Recipes

Chapter 15 of this book is a collection of freezer-worthy recipes. They have all been freezer tested. Chapter 11 is sample outline for cooking 30 meals in one day. You could use the 30 day outline for a guided first experience. You could, however, substitute your own recipes and jump right in. Be kind to yourself, though, and choose your recipes carefully. Be careful not to choose too many time consuming, labor intensive recipes.

The first time I got the bug to try putting dinners in the freezer I decided on 30 for no other reason than 30 days makes a month. I chose 30 recipes and worked and worked and worked. I accomplished the task but I was exhausted at the end of the day and I still had to clean up. I did not look forward to the experience again.

Preparing 30 recipes is too time consuming and makes for an experience you will not likely revisit. Plan for 30 meals, but choose only 15 recipes. Adjust each recipe to make at least two meals for those for whom you are cooking. Even if you double or triple your recipes, it takes virtually no more effort to make two of pretty much any recipe than it does to make one.

It is important that you freeze **meal-size**, not recipe-size. If you are cooking for one or for two or for a small family, perhaps a recipe will already make two meals. You won't need to adjust the recipe. You could cut the recipe down, but why? It takes no less time to make half a recipe. Make the entire recipe and divide into meal-sized portions. If it makes more than two meals consider this a bonus! If you are cooking for 4 and the recipe is for 6, you will need increase the recipe by half. If you are cooking for 6 and the recipe is for 6, you will need to double the recipe. Whatever your family size, adjust each recipe so that it makes at least two meals.

You may be eating the same thing twice in a month but you would be surprised just how often we really do make the same favorites. Next time you can choose 15 completely different recipes. The dinners you place in the freezer will keep for three to six months, so if you overlap your 30 meal cooking days you will increase the variety of meals you have to choose from.

The *30 Meals in One Day* computer program allows you to easily **adjust recipe sizes**, as well as many other time saving functions. Please refer to page 14 for more information.

Recipe Cards

Whether you use recipes from this book, from your own collection or a combination of both, you will want to put each recipe on a separate 4 x 6 card. I know, I know. You have your favorite recipe collection and you like it just the way it is, thank you very much. Perhaps it is all neatly bound in the notebook grandma gave you, or perhaps it is in 14 different cookbooks but you are so familiar with them you can flip right to them whenever you want. Maybe you are completely comfortable with that cardboard box of miscellaneous recipes that you dig through each time you need a recipe.

Each of those methods has its benefits, but when you are preparing 30 meals all in one day you do not want to be flipping back and forth in books or binders or digging in your beloved box. Trust me on this, your cooking day will not only be easier but will be more rewarding if you have a separate recipe card for each recipe you prepare. It will be *easier* because you will need recipes near the slow cooker, recipes near the stove, and recipes on the counter. As the dishes are prepared and moved to the table to cool, the recipe card follows, so you can refer to it when you label the package for the freezer. It will be *rewarding* because as you finish a recipe and it has cooled, been packaged, and labeled you get to put that recipe card into the beautiful DONE pile. *Oh,* the satisfaction of watching that pile grow!

Save guess work in the future by writing how many meals your version of the recipe will make, directly on the recipe card. Mark on each card the number of freezer bags or containers you will need in order to package the number of meals that recipe will make. It is also helpful to write on the top, right corner the type of cooking method required for the recipe: Slow Cooker, Oven, StoveTop or Assemble.

The **30 Meals in One Day** computer program will **print recipes** and save you a bucket of time. Print and use the recipes you need, then either file them away or toss them! You can print a new selection of recipes next time, if you desire. See page 14 for more information.

Fully Cooked vs. Ready to Bake

Recipes can generally be divided into two categories: 1. *Fully Cooked*, and 2. *Assembled and Ready to Bake*.

Fully Cooked is generally anything that you would normally cook completely on the stove top or slow cooker and put on the table. Some examples of Fully Cooked recipes are, chili, soup and spaghetti sauce. These recipes you will cook completely, allow to cool and package them for your freezer. To serve, you will thaw them, heat to piping hot and serve.

Assembled and Ready to Bake includes such recipes as lasagna, chicken enchiladas and meat loaf. These recipes you will prepare just to the point of baking, then you will package them for the freezer. To serve, you will thaw them, then bake and serve.

Cooking Methods

Before choosing 15 recipes to prepare, you must first divide them according to cooking method and/or time required to prepare each. Slow Cooker recipes, Oven recipes, StoveTop recipes and Assemble recipes.

Your recipe list should very nearly consist of:

✐ 2 Slow Cooker recipes

✐ 2 Oven recipes

✐ 2 StoveTop recipes

✐ 9 Assemble recipes

This is a *general* rule. The number of each will probably vary, at times. Just be sure to limit the total to 15. Don't choose more Slow Cooker and Oven recipes than are physically possible in a day, and avoid choosing too many labor intensive StoveTop recipes.

Choose your recipes carefully. You do not want to overload yourself with 15 labor intensive recipes that will take more than a day to make.

Choose 2 Slow Cooker recipes

The number of Slow Cooker recipes you can choose depends on the number of slow cookers you have and the time required for each recipe.

Generally, Slow Cooker recipes can be cooked on High for 4 to 6 hours or on Low for 8 to 10 hours. This is not a rule, just a guideline. If you desire to cook two recipes in one day and both recipes give you the option of cooking on High for 4 to 6 hours or less, you can probably accomplish this. Choose only one recipe if your recipe requires 8 to 10 hours and you have only one slow cooker.

If you have the opportunity to do some preparation the day before your cooking day, consider starting a recipe in the slow cooker before you go to bed. Choose a recipe with a Low 8 to 10 hours or longer cooking time. By the time you get up in the morning you'll already have one recipe cooked and ready to be cooled and packaged for the freezer. You can immediately start a new recipe in the slow cooker.

It is feasible that you could cook four Slow Cooker recipes with only one slow cooker if you choose two Low 8 to 10 hour recipes and two High 4 to 6 hour or less recipes. Cook one of the Low 8 to 10 hour recipes the night before cooking day. First thing on cooking day replace that recipe with a High 4 to 6 hour recipe. When it is done, immediately replace it with another short cooking recipe. Then before you go to bed at night, put the last of the four recipes, a long cooking recipe, in the slow cooker. This will be your final recipe of the day.

Choose 2 Oven recipes
Oven recipes are cooked in the oven before freezing. These recipes can require lengthy baking times. They can also be those recipes that you desire to bake prior to freezing to pro- vide you with the convenience of thawing a completely cooked meal that can be quickly heated and served. Bake these on cooking day, cool, and freeze. To serve them, you will simply thaw them, then heat and eat! Oven recipes do NOT include lasagna, chicken enchiladas, or ham and pota- toes and the like. These recipes will be assembled, then frozen before baking. Repeatedly baking or heating them can cause this type of recipe to be dry, overdone and/or tough.

Some ground beef recipes, especially meatloaf and meat-balls, can get tough with overheating. This type of recipe will only be baked just before serving.

Choose 2 StoveTop recipes

StoveTop recipes include those recipes that are prepared on a burner on the stove top. These recipes tend to be time con-suming and labor intensive, so don't choose too many of them. Limit yourself to only two labor intensive StoveTop recipes. Depending on the recipe, you could probably pre-pare more of this type, but work with two before you exper-iment with more. If you choose too many StoveTop recipes you may not have time to complete them all, making the process last more than a day. If your first experience with cooking many meals on the same day is too difficult, you may never want to try it again.

Choose 9 Assemble recipes

Assemble recipes require very little or no cooking in prepa-ration to get them to the point they can be frozen. These recipes will be frozen prior to heating or baking. Recipes like **Chicken Enchiladas** and **Lasagna** will be layered in a foil baking pan and frozen. You will bake these on the day they will be served. Recipes such as **Tuna Bow Ties** and **Cheesy Ham and Potatoes**, will be assembled and frozen in freezer bags. To serve, you will first thaw them, then pour into a dish and either bake or microwave. These recipes will be the bulk of your cooking day. They are the least time consuming, the most rewarding and are just as tasty as the others.

Chapter 5

Lists That Will Make Your Life Easier

List Chosen Recipes

As you choose your recipes, make a list of the recipe titles. This list will become your "menu" and will help you remember what you have in your freezer. Write down how many of each recipe you put in the freezer, or put a square or circle in front of the title for each meal you put in the freezer. As you take a meal from your freezer, mark off the circle or square. This way you'll always know what is in your freezer.

Although dating each meal is a good idea, you may find it even more helpful to date the list. When I forget about something in the freezer and then I find it later at the bottom of my freezer and the date tells me it is a year old I think, "Yep, it's a year old." With a date at the top of the list, you can always tell what is in your freezer and how long it has been there. Add to the list as you add other things to your freezer. Always add the correct date.

As a meal is removed from the freezer, be sure to check it off the list. This way you will always know what you have in the freezer and you will be able to tell how soon you need to replenish your supply of frozen meals.

The *30 Meals in One Day* computer program will make this list for you. It will print out your List of Chosen Recipes or **Menu**, complete with the number of each meal you freeze and date that you put it in the freezer. See page 14 for more information.

Following is a sample list that you can make for yourself or print from the computer program:

TODAY'S DATE

☐☐   Brown Sugar Pork Ribs
☐☐   Cream Cheese Chicken
☐☐   Oven Stew
☐☐   Candied Chicken
☐☐☐   Taco Soup
☐☐   Chicken Tortellini Soup
☐☐☐☐ Spaghetti
☐☐   Cheese Manicotti
☐☐   Simply Lasagna
☐☐   BBQ Beef and Biscuits
☐☐   Meat Loaf and Potatoes
☐☐   Tortilla Chicken
☐☐   Ham and Chicken Roll-Ups
☐☐   Cheesy Ham and Potatoes
☐☐   Tuna Bow Ties

This list actually has two purposes. The first, of course, is to help you keep track of what is in the freezer. The second is it becomes your "menu" of sorts. Do you ever feel frustrated about the question, "What's for dinner?" This list will make answering this question easier for you. Simply choose a meal from the list.

You could present your list to family members and let them choose what is for dinner. Just be sure to only show one family member the menu choices on any particular day. Everyone who looks at the menu will surely disagree over which of the yummy choices will be for dinner!

Shopping List

Making a shopping list is an absolute must. If you are one who wouldn't dream of shopping without a list you will be comfortable with this. If you are one who likes to go to the store and "wing it," well, don't. You are sure to miss some little thing that will either prevent you from preparing the recipe you started, or cause you to interrupt your momentum to run to the store to retrieve the required item. In the long run, a list saves you time and frustration.

Start with your 15 recipes in front you. You will also need a pencil and a sheet of notebook paper or something similar in size. Forget the skinny little shopping list paper. You need to be able to *see* everything you are shopping for.

Group the items on your list by category. For example, list all the meat on the first lines on the left side of the page. Make hash marks as you go. One hash mark for each chicken breast, one hash mark for each pound of ground beef, one hash mark for each pork chop, and one hash mark for each pound of spare ribs. Next group all dairy products. Use one hash mark for each cup of milk, sour cream and so on. Group all canned goods. Use one hash mark for each can. Be sure to write down the number of ounces, if it is an unusual amount or if it is a can of something that comes in multiple sizes. Group all frozen foods. Use one hash mark for each box, can or bag, noting the ounces or size when necessary. Group all pasta. Use one hash mark for each type and size bag or box of pasta. Group all fresh produce. Keep track of vegetables by the piece or by the pound. For example, use one hash mark for each onion and one hash mark for each pound of baby carrots.

Group all packaging materials, and any other categories you need. Once you fill up one side of the paper with groups, make a second column of groups on the right hand side of the same side of the paper. Continue to add ingredients to the list as you go through each recipe card.

The **30 Meals in One Day** computer program will make this process simple. As you choose your recipes, the computer program simultaneously generates your shipping list. When you are finished deciding on a menu, your shopping list can be printed out, already in categories, and you are ready to head to the store!

Following is a sample of a shopping list you could make for yourself or print a similar one from the computer program.

Meat
ground beef ~~HHH~~ //
chicken breast ~~HHH~~ ~~HHH~~
stew meat ~~HHH~~
pork roast /

Dairy
sour cream //
cream cheese ///
Cheddar cheese //
Mozzarella ///

Pasta
manicotti
lasagna
bow ties (16-oz)
noodles (12-oz) //

Seasonings
taco seasoning //
soy sauce
worcestershire sauce
vinegar

Produce
green bell pepper //
celery /
carrots //
onions ~~HHH~~

Frozen
hash browns (24-oz) //
petite peas (16-oz) //
mixed vegetables (16-oz) //

Canned Goods
cream of chicken soup ~~HHH~~
spaghetti sauce (26-oz) ///
canned milk (12-oz) //

Other
French fried onions //

Packaging
foil pans (9x9) ///
gallon freezer bags
extra heavy foil

This method will help prevent you from overlooking needed items. As you come to each department of the grocery store you will be able to get everything on the list in that particular category. It is more likely that you will be to the end of the list by the time you get to the end of the store! How frustrating it is to realize that you have overlooked few things and now have to go back through the store to find them.

If you are really feeling organized, you can list your groups in the order you come upon them in the store. This is not necessary but it certainly streamlines the shopping effort. Most grocery stores have a map of the layout of the items in that store. You may want to get one and plan your list around the format of the store.

If you already have an item there is no need to add it to your grocery list. Just be sure you do not "use" the same item from your cupboard in more than one recipe. For example, if you need soy sauce for 4 recipes, make sure that the amount of soy sauce you do have will be sufficient for all four recipes.

You will be packaging your dinners in freezer pans, freezer bags, and plastic freezer containers. Decide which method you prefer for each recipe and count how many disposable pans, gallon freezer bags, quart freezer bags, and plastic freezer containers you will need. Don't forget the extra heavy foil.

After you have made your shopping list, arrange your recipes in the order you will be preparing them. Arrange the cards with the Slow Cooker recipes first, then Oven, then Stove-Top, and then the Assemble recipes. Arrange the Slow Cooker recipes with the shortest cooking time recipe first. Arrange the remainder of the recipes in order starting with the one that takes the longest and ending with the easiest one. It can be discouraging to get to the end of the cooking day and find that you have a complicated recipe still to make. Prepare the hardest recipes or the recipes you least enjoy making first. When you complete recipe number 14 and you find that number 15 is an easy recipe or one you truly enjoy making you will be so glad you took a minute to put your recipes in order before starting!

Chapter 6

The Day Before

Shop

Your recipes are chosen and your list is made. You're ready to shop. The very first time I got the bug to put 30 meals in my freezer I was so excited. I wanted to go shopping and come home and get started RIGHT NOW. Don't do that. You do not want to begin your cooking day with a huge shopping excursion. Shopping can wear a person out and if you start cooking that same day you are likely to run out of steam before you get to recipe number 15. You will want to start out the cooking day fresh. So, DO NOT shop on cooking day, but do try to shop the day before. There are plenty of things you can do after you shop to prepare for cooking day. The preparations will make your cooking day go smoothly. Before you leave for the store, clear everything off your counters and table that you will not need on cooking day. Now you are ready to go shopping.

Arrange the Goods

When you get home do NOT put everything away. There is no need to find room in your cupboards for those things when you are going to be using them all tomorrow anyway. Refrigerate anything perishable but leave the rest out. Arrange all the goods wherever you will need them first. Stack all the canned goods near the can opener. Anything you know you will be using at the stove, such as pasta, put near the stove. If it is an ingredient you will be mixing or assembling at the counter, arrange it to the side of the counter.

There will be plenty of things that you already have in your cupboards that you will also need. Get these things out so they will be handy and available the second you need them. You may have a lot of items in food storage. Retrieve them now so that you won't have to make a trip to your storage each time you need one. Arrange everything neatly on the counter with the labels turned so that you can easily identify each.

After you empty the bags of groceries, don't fold up the bags. Put one brown paper grocery bag near the can opener, one beside the counter, one near the stove, one near the table, and anywhere else you will be working. The idea is to make sure you have the capability of throwing things away without having to take more than a step or two. This will keep your work space tidier and easier to work in and it will save you steps. When you are cooking all day, any step you can save is a plus.

Choose a place that you will package your dinners for the freezer, such as the kitchen table. This is the spot to place all your freezer bags, boxes and foil pans. Put the freezer foil and your marker and/or labels on the table. Also put the non-stick cooking spray and some trivets on the table. After you prepare a recipe and it needs to cool, you can set it on a trivet on the table to cool. When it is cool you will have everything you need within easy reach to package, label, and freeze it, without stopping to search for necessary items.

Chop the Vegetables

After you come home from shopping and have arranged the goods, you may want to make some further preparations for cooking day. If you have the time and the desire, chop the vegetables. Count how many onions you need for all recipes, and dice or chop them and place them in bags or in a bowl, cover, and refrigerate. You can take care of any other vegetable preparation your recipes call for. Peel and slice the carrots, slice the onions, dice the bell peppers, slice the mushrooms, etc. You will probably need more chopped onions than any other vegetable. Even if you only chop your onions the day before, it will be a huge help to you on cooking day. A big bowl of chopped onions on cooking day is a beautiful thing!

Shred the Cheese

If you did not purchase your cheese already shredded, count the number of cups of cheese that are needed for all recipes. Use your food processor if you have one. If you do not you will find it helpful to shred your cheese the day before you cook. Put it into a bowl or resealable plastic bags and put it in the refrigerator. Sometimes I have noticed that shredded cheese at the grocery store is the same price or only slightly more than a block of cheese. In this case, I always buy the shredded. The time saved is valuable. You may want to buy the cheese already shredded no matter how much extra the cost. Whatever method you choose and are comfortable with, shredded cheese on cooking day is a beautiful thing!

Cook the Chicken

Refrigerate all the meat except the chicken. Separate all the recipes that call for cooked chicken and count the number of chicken pieces required. It is a close guess to say that one chicken breast equals one cup of cooked chicken. Of course, chicken breast sizes vary but as an average this is a good rule of thumb. Put the counted pieces of chicken in a big pot with a piece of celery broken in half, a large washed but unpeeled carrot with the ends removed and broken in half, and a large peeled and quartered onion. Cover all ingredients with water and add a few peppercorns and some salt. Cook the chicken until it is done. Remove the chicken to cool.

While the chicken is cooling, either strain the broth or just remove and discard the cooked vegetables and peppercorns. SAVE THE BROTH. You can use it in any recipe that calls for chicken broth. If there is still broth remaining after you've prepared all the recipes that call for chicken broth, you can add some more chopped vegetables and noodles to make a fabulous chicken soup. Why pay for canned chicken broth when you can make tastier broth just from cooking the chicken you need cooked anyway.

When the chicken is cool enough to work with, either use scissors to chop it or shred it into a large bowl. Cover the bowl and refrigerate it until tomorrow when you cook. A big bowl of cooked and chopped or shredded chicken on cooking day is a beautiful thing!

Thaw all the Meat

Perhaps you have meat in your freezer you will be cooking on cooking day. Be sure to get it out of the freezer in time to thaw for cooking day. Be sure to thaw all meat in the refrigerator. You can thaw and refreeze meat without consequence if the meat is never allowed to come to room temperature. Meat that is allowed to come to room temperature can allow harmful bacteria to grow which can cause illness. Always thaw meat in the refrigerator.

While certainly not mandatory, all the advanced preparation you can do will make your cooking day much easier. Waking up on the day you are going to put 30 meals in your freezer, with these preparations already accomplished, is truly a beautiful thing!

Chapter 7

Cooking Day

Perhaps the most important preparation you can make for cooking day is to arrange your day. Choose a day that you have no obligations that will interrupt you and take you away from the kitchen. Eliminate the need to run errands, have someone else drive car pool, arrange for someone to help you with the children, don't answer the phone! (okay, except for emergencies). Combine children and cook with a friend, or trade cooking and tending days. Cook one day while she tends your children and then you can tend her children on another day while she cooks.

Sometimes you will not be able to complete all, or perhaps any, of the food preparation the day before. If this is the case, the Chapter 6 preparations are what you will do first. Clear every unnecessary thing off the counters and table. Set out the brown paper grocery bag trash containers. Start your slow cooker. You'll want to get every working moment you can from your slow cooker. Cook, cool and chop or shred the chicken. Chop the vegetables, especially all the onions. Shred all the cheese you will need. You don't want to have to stop to peel and chop an onion, or shred cheese, or cook, cool and shred chicken each time you need some. Stopping to perform these tasks over and over during your cooking day is a time waster, a momentum breaker, a motivation killer! Do these tasks once and be done with them.

Your slow cooker is already working. Now fill the oven. Put both recipes in the oven if they will fit at the same time. If not, start with the recipe with the shortest cooking time. Next start the StoveTop recipes. Don't make both StoveTop recipes at the same time. They are time consuming and labor intensive. Just babysit one recipe at a time. While the Stove-Top recipe is cooking you can begin assembling recipes at the counter. Remember to keep an eye on the stove top. Keep a running list of what is cooking and the times they are done or need an ingredient added. If the slow cooker is done in 3 hours, write down "Slow Cooker" or the recipe title. Next to that, write **what time it will be** in 3 hours, say 11:30. Be sure to write the time the recipe is done! If you simply write 3 hours, you are sure to wonder what time you started.

When you have the slow cooker working, the oven working and a recipe started on the stove top, you'll be ready to begin assembling recipes. Arrange the chosen Assemble recipes in the order you plan to make them. Start with the most difficult recipe or the one you least enjoy making. End with the easiest recipe or the recipe you enjoy making the most. Don't succumb to thinking that you should break your-self in gently on cooking day by making the easiest recipes first! If you put off making the most difficult recipe until the end...after you've prepared 14 other recipes...how likely will you be to actually make that difficult recipe? Be kind to yourself and prepare the difficult recipe first while you are fresh. The easy recipe is your final recipe, sort of your reward. You complete the easy one and you're finished!

Before you start assembling the first recipe, look ahead to the second. Does it call for something that can be cooking while you assemble number one? For example, if the second recipe calls for pasta, start cooking the pasta while you assemble the first recipe. Use a timer so you don't have to remember when it is done. You may be finished assembling it before the pasta for recipe number two is done. If not, the timer will tell you when the pasta is done. You can drain it and it can sit in the sink and wait for you while you finish the first recipe. When finished with the first, move on to the second. The pasta is ready to go and all you need to do is assemble the ingredients, but before you begin to assemble it look ahead to the third. If it needs something that you can start while making the second, start it. This way you stay one recipe ahead of the assembly process and are always ready to move on to the next.

As recipes are done, move them to the table to be packaged for the freezer. The recipe card travels along with the food so that you can refer to it for any cooking instructions you want to include on the label.

Anything layered, such as enchiladas, will be assembled in the container it will be frozen in. These dishes can immediately be covered with foil and labeled. Be sure to include the baking time and temperature.

When you adapt your own recipes for the freezer you may need to add 50% to the recommended baking time. For example, normally when you make lasagna, you start with warm noodles and warm sauce, then when the layering is complete, you place the already warm meal into the oven. Perhaps your recipe calls for 30 minutes baking time. If you place a recently thawed lasagna from the freezer in the oven, it starts out cold. It will require more baking time. Adding 50% more baking time would be adding 15 minutes. It should be hot and ready after 45 minutes, but this is a *general* rule, certainly not an exact science.

Once your meals are labeled they are ready to be frozen. Put the recipe card in the *done* pile. When the StoveTop and Oven recipes are done you can move them to the table on trivets to cool. Recipe cards travel right along with them. If you have other recipes for the stove top or oven, start them. If not, continue to assemble recipes at the counter, cooking pasta, etc. as you go. When the meals cooling on the table are cool, put meal-sized portions into freezer containers or freezer bags, label them and they are ready to be frozen.

In Chapter 11, a sample 30-meal, 15-recipe cooking day is completely mapped out for you, step by step. If all 15 recipes appeal to you, start with this. Or substitute recipes with similar cooking requirements for the recipes that don't appeal to you and stick closely to the outline.

There is no disguising the fact that preparing 30 meals from 15 different recipes requires your undivided attention for a significant amount of the day. It is not overly difficult but it *will* require several hours to accomplish. However, it is important to remember that the time and effort you spend today will result in one day of freedom for each meal you place in the freezer. Also important to note is that preparing many meals in one day will consume much less time than preparing the same number of meals individually.

After you have accomplished 30 meals in one day, your subsequent experiences will flow more smoothly and will be less time consuming. You will settle into your own method and discover your own shortcuts.

I have cooked with many different people. Some I knew before our cooking experience and some I did not know before I helped them cook. Based on my experience, I have found that there are two main types of cooks. I affectionately call them the Chaos Queens and the Neat Freaks.

The Chaos Queens are comfortable in their chaos. The Chaos Queens like to leave the groceries in the grocery bags and retrieve just what they want when they need it. This defeats the whole save-every-unnecessary-step theory. If you have to go to the grocery bag and then to the can opener each time you need a can of soup, you have wasted a lot of effort and time in the course of a cooking day. Throwing away boxes or wrappers immediately is okay with the Chaos Queen, but it's also okay with them if they get thrown away later. They may have two sets of measuring spoons and cups, but part of one set is probably in the dishwasher or in the toy box. This is okay with them. They get over it as they go. A little time lost here because they had to rinse and dry out the measuring cup so they can measure ingredients is tolerated. Tolerated but not helpful.

Chaos is okay on a meal-by-meal basis but it really doesn't work when you are cooking 15 recipes for 30 meals in just one day. You must be somewhat organized. You will become frustrated and lose your momentum if you have to stop and search for the measuring cups, or the vinegar, or the soy sauce each time you need it.

The Neat Freaks are completely uncomfortable with anything out of order. I have noticed that Neat Freaks have the most difficulty adapting to the 30 meals in one day effort. They feel the need to wash, dry and put away every spoon, bowl and measuring cup as well as put away every salt shaker and bottle of soy sauce as it is used.

Many times, while cooking with a neat freak, I have set down a measuring cup and when I reached for the same one 3 minutes later, it was gone. I would look around for it and find it either *in the dishwasher* or *back in the drawer!* Choose something that you use a lot, let's say the salt. Now let's say you will be using the salt 12 times on cooking day. Let me demonstrate the loss of time for you. Walk to the cupboard and get out the salt, walk to the counter to add it to a recipe, then walk back to cupboard and put it away. Repeat this 12 times and you will see what a lot of wasted effort is involved in putting everything away each time.

Neat Freaks also have a hard time using the same bowl to mix up one recipe after another was made in it. They feel it must be washed, rinsed, dried and put away before it can be used again. If you feel this way, let me say this gently. It is okay to reuse a bowl that has been used to mix another recipe in it first. It does not have cooties. Nothing has been in it long enough to spoil or be dirty in any way. There may be times when the first recipe has flavors left in the bowl that will collide with the next recipe. In this case, a quick rinse will do. Of course, anything that has touched raw meat must be washed immediately.

If you are a Neat Freak you must "let your hair down" just one day. Let things stay out until their use is over for just one day. All 29 other days of the month you can have complete order in your kitchen. If you are a Chaos Queen, "put your hair up" just one day and be better organized. It will save you time and you will not regret it.

Whether you are a Chaos Queen, or a Neat Freak, or somewhere in the middle, seek to have organized chaos in your kitchen on cooking day. Things may appear chaotic but don't let them get sloppy. Keep things out that you need, put them away when they've been used for the last time, wash a little as you go, take out and replace trash bags as they fill. Don't succumb to interruptions. You will be much happier and your experience will go much more smoothly and pleasantly.

Chapter 8

Packaging for the Freezer

Your freezer packaging options are many. They include reusable plastic freezer containers, resealable freezer bags, and disposable aluminum pans. Each of these comes in a wide variety of sizes. Using containers designed for the freezer ensures that your meals will come out of the freezer as tasty as they went in.

Any food that is exposed to the air is subject to freezer burn. As food freezes, the air draws the moisture out. Notice any frost on your food? This is freezer burn. The moisture has been drawn out by the air and forms ice crystals. Chicken and other meats turn white and rubbery. Pasta gets dry, white and eventually crumbles. This is freezer burn. It can be prevented by eliminating as much air as possible from your packaged dinners.

Manufacturers are continually coming out with new and better products for freezing and storing food. Keep an eye out for new products that will improve your life and make your meal preparation and freezing easier.

Reusable Plastic Freezer Containers

Plastic freezer containers can be used many times. Be sure to purchase only the type that are labeled freezer, microwave and dishwasher safe. With these you can package single servings to family sized servings and most any size in between. They can go from freezer to microwave to dishwasher and then right back to the freezer again with zero damage. Being able to microwave meals is a huge time saver when you have very limited time to serve a meal.

Plastic freezer containers are especially handy for soups and liquid recipes like spaghetti sauce since the rigid sides of the container provide more stability. You can write the name of the recipe and any cooking instructions right on the lid or you can attach a label. If you use a permanent marker to label the lid, any scouring powder will remove the ink and you will be able to relabel it each time it is used. Labels are easily soaked off.

When you use this type of container, leave 1/4-inch head-space so the food has room to expand as it freezes. Other-wise, the food will expand and pop the lid off in the freezer. Air causes freezer burn so try to never let chicken or other meat be exposed to the air, even within a freezer container. If the container has room left after you have placed the desired amount of food in the container, press a piece of plastic wrap onto the surface of the food and replace the lid. This will help protect the food from the air and subsequent freezer burn.

This type of container is especially useful for freezing single servings. Having an assortment of single servings such as **Sweet and Sour Chicken** over rice, **Beef Stroganoff** over noodles, **Cream Cheese Chicken** over mashed potatoes, **Taco Soup**, etc. will make lunch easy and enjoyable. They make a welcome change from another boring sandwich for lunch. They are easy to take from the freezer in the morning for you or others in your life who carry lunch to work. They are also handy for days when the family is scattered and only one or two are home for dinner.

Resealable Freezer Bags

Resealable freezer bags don't come in as many sizes as freez-er containers but they are probably the most inexpensive, convenient and easy to use. Almost any meal that does not have to be layered can be frozen in a resealable freezer bag.

Individual servings can be frozen in pint bags, small family portions in quart bags and larger family portions in gallon bags. Even meals that end up in a pan, but are not layered, can be frozen in a bag. They can be placed in a baking dish when you are ready to heat and serve the meal.

There are quite a few brands of resealable freezer bags. Be sure to get good quality freezer bags with good thick plastic and solid seams. Some of the lower quality bags tend to break at the seams and sometimes the zipper doesn't line up. Buy the best brand that you can that is on sale. Seems there is always one on sale.

Label your freezer bag **before** you put the food into it. The food, especially anything cold, tends to make the bag sweat. It is difficult to write on anything wet, even with the best of permanent markers. Labels don't cooperate under sweaty conditions either.

When you are ready to put a meal into a gallon freezer bag, open the bag and fold the top couple of inches of the bag back over itself. This will give the bag stability, making it easy to fill. The bag will stand up and stay open by itself. Hold on to one side as you fill the bag so that it doesn't fall over when full of food. Folding the bag back will also make it easier to protect the zipper of the bag. This prevents the tedious and messy cleanup job of cleaning any drips off the zipper so that it will seal properly.

To fill a quart or pint freezer bag, use a canning funnel. You will find that a standard canning funnel, the size used for narrow mouth canning jars, fits perfectly in the top of a quart bag. You can hold the top of the bag right around the bowl of the funnel and filling the bag is a breeze. A standard serving spoon fits nicely into the mouth of the funnel if you are using a spoon.

Whichever size of freezer bag you use, be sure to press all the air out of the bag before you seal it. This is a very important step since air causes freezer burn. Any air left in the bag dries out the food during storage. The moisture is drawn out of the food and forms a frost in the package. If all the air is pressed out and the bag is touching the food, freezer burn can be prevented. Fold any unused portion of the bag under the food and make a flat, stackable package.

If you are unsure about the amount of recipes like soup, stew or chili, to put into a freezer bag, measure each family member's portion. You can give a pretty close guess to how much each family member eats. You've been feeding them for how long?! Place food, such as **Taco Soup**, into a serving bowl to represent a specific family member's portion. Then measure the food with a measuring cup. Write down the amount. Do this for each member of the family. Some may eat an entire bowl full, others may eat half a bowl. If members of your family normally want seconds or thirds, add this to the total. Also factor in your desire for leftovers and perhaps the likelihood of a stray dinner guest. Write the total right on your recipe card. You'll never again wonder how much you should measure into a freezer bag for a family sized meal. You could also determine the total amount that will go into the freezer bag using water, if you don't want to measure actual food.

To measure something like spaghetti sauce, measure the real thing. For example, using a measuring cup, pour a portion of spaghetti sauce onto a plate to determine the approximate amount each member of the family is likely to eat. Add these amounts for your family members and record the total. You will probably be freezing a lesser amount of spaghetti sauce than you will something like chili. Chili is a meal by itself and will take up more room than spaghetti sauce that will be served over noodles. Perhaps a family-sized portion of chili will be frozen in a gallon bag while a family sized portion of spaghetti sauce may easily fit into a quart bag.

To measure something that will be poured into a baking dish after it is thawed, like **Tuna Bow Ties** or **Cheesy Ham and Potatoes**, fill a baking pan with the amount your family will eat, measure it and put that amount into the bag. Put the total measurement right on your recipe card so you will know each time you make it how much goes into each freezer bag.

If, after serving a recipe, you notice that you had way too much or not quite enough, be sure to adjust your notes on your recipe card so that it will be near perfect next time.

Disposable Foil Pans

Disposable foil pans come in about any size you desire - single servings all the way to large pot luck size and every size in between. Some even come with neat and tidy foil-lined tops that you lay on top of the pan and then crimp the edges over. Don't be concerned about the shape of the pan. Rather, choose the pans that will contain the number of servings you need for one meal.

After filling the pan with food, either cover with the foil-lined top, or cover it tightly with extra heavy foil. It is not necessary to wrap the pan entirely, just cover the top and crimp over the edges. Press the foil right down on top of the food to eliminate as much air as possible. Remember, air is not your friend in the freezer. Write the name of the recipe and any cooking instructions right on the foil or foil-lined cover. Labels attach easily if you prefer them.

Another option for freezing layered dinners is to line a baking dish with extra heavy foil, making sure there is enough excess to completely cover the food when the dish is full. Arrange the meal in the foil and seal tightly. Place the entire foil wrapped meal, dish and all, in the freezer and allow it to freeze solid. Now you can remove the foil wrapped meal from the dish and stack it in the freezer, which frees up your baking dish. When you are ready to serve the meal, unwrap the frozen meal and place it in the dish to thaw and then bake. For speedy clean up, place the meal - foil and all - in the dish. Thaw and bake as usual. Simply toss the foil and there is no dish to wash.

Presentation is sometimes as important as the meal. A foil-lined dish or a foil baking pan will certainly ruin the presentation. In this case you would want to remove the foil.

Since it will take a while to wait for each recipe to freeze before you can have your dish back, you will want to use foil baking pans that are the sizes of your baking dishes. Cover the meals in foil, and freeze. You can easily place the meal in a baking dish when ready to serve the meal. Make sure the foil pan is the same size as your baking dish. Remove the pan while the food is frozen.

Chapter 9

The Freezer

The meals you place in your freezer will remain delicious for three to six months if packaged properly and if your freezer is maintained at zero degrees or lower. It is important that each meal be cooled *completely* before putting it into the freezer. Putting 30 meals of warm food into your freezer can cause the temperature to rise within the freezer and the quality of the food you already have in the freezer could be compromised. Also, the freezer motor could be overworked and could be damaged. If you have only a small freezer in your refrigerator, you may even want to put some of your packaged meals into the refrigerator and allow them to be completely cold before adding them to the freezer.

If you have only a small freezer in your refrigerator, your challenge to fit 30 meals is greater. You will need to stack your meals carefully, and take advantage of every available space in your freezer. You may need to have only one box of ice cream at a time in your freezer for a couple of weeks until half of the meals are gone.

The space in a refrigerator freezer is deceptive. You really can get a lot more into a refrigerator freezer than it appears you can. Also, remember that you are freezing meal-size not recipe-size and that you are not freezing bulky pans or dishes. Food in a plastic bag takes up a lot less space than the same food in a baking or serving dish.

Your job is definitely easier if you have an upright or chest style freezer. Each of these types of freezers has its bonuses and downfalls. The upright freezer makes it easier to stack and find your meals, however, each time you open the door the cold "falls out" and your freezer will have to work harder, especially when you bombard it with many meals in one day. Having the cold "fall out" on a daily use basis as you get out a bag of peas or a box of ice cream is not harmful. The freezer motor is designed to keep the interior of the freezer at zero degrees. However, if you open the freezer door and let the cold "fall out" 30 times when adding room temperature food, you risk having your freezer motor go on strike! A solution for this is to accumulate five or six meals and open your freezer fewer times. You could also collect the meals in the refrigerator to give them a chance to get cool before you put them in the freezer.

A chest style freezer contains the cold better as the cold will never fall out. However, the challenge is greater to stack things in a manner that makes the meals easy to retrieve without you falling in! There is a relatively simple solution to this, I have discovered, as I am in possession of a chest style freezer.

The first time I prepared 30 meals and desired to arrange them in my freezer, I was at first stumped until I noticed my kids' toy assortment in the garage. All the tennis balls, baseball gloves and swim fins were arranged in a three tier, stacking toy bin or utility bin. It consists of three baskets, stacked on top of each other with the front of each open to accommodate the toys. I dumped the toys on the garage floor (someone else can put them away - I'm cooking!) and lowered the whole thing into my freezer. It works beautifully!! The three baskets provide plenty of room for me to stack all the meals and all are easily accessible. These stacking, open shelf baskets can be found where organizer containers are sold. They can also be found at the large office supply stores.

The idea is to create vertical space in your chest style freezer. It is not important what you use, just that you create vertical space. A three tier stacking toy bin works great but so does a small plastic or metal bookshelf. Plastic crates, turned on their sides work well, too. Crates create cubicle vertical space. Choose crates that are not so big that the stacking area inside each crate is too high.

Plastic coated wire shelves are convenient to create vertical space. They snap together securely and come in many sizes. This allows you to create different configurations for your specific needs and freezer space.

For some, it is a common practice to fill cardboard boxes and stack them up in a chest freezer. This makes anything in the bottom box very difficult to retrieve. Don't sabotage your hard work by filling boxes and stacking them one on top of the other, making the meals inconvenient and difficult to remove. You will use more space in your freezer if your food is accessible.

Whatever the style of your freezer, first spread the meals out in as much of a single layer as possible. Allow them to freeze or at least get very cold before stacking them on top of each other. Any liquid filled freezer bags, such as chicken soup, chili, taco soup or spaghetti sauce should be almost entirely frozen before stacking. Weight on the top of one of these liquid filled bags could cause too much pressure on the seam and cause it to break. Then you'll have a soupy mess in your freezer. You might also desire to avoid stacking like meals together. Try putting an assortment of meals on each shelf.

Remember the list of recipes (Menu) you made when you chose your recipes? Use this list to keep track of what you have prepared and placed in your freezer. You can also mark the list with the location of each. Perhaps it is on the second shelf on the right. Or perhaps it is in the bottom blue crate.

As a meal is removed from the freezer, be sure to check it off the list. This way you will always know what you have in the freezer and be able to tell how soon you need to replenish your supply. Keeping a list of what is in your freezer and the location of each, will make finding and using what you have prepared a breeze, regardless of your freezer size or style.

Chapter 10

Thawing

Meals in freezer bags that have thawed, can be conveniently poured into baking dishes for the oven, into dishes to be heated in the microwave, or into pans for heating on the stove top.

Meals frozen in foil baking pans will need to be thawed before baking, in order to be ready to serve in the baking time recommended on the recipe. Even then, the times listed for each recipe represent an *approximate* baking time. The actual temperature of the food and how thoroughly thawed the meal is, will determine the actual length of baking time required.

Frozen meals should be thawed in the refrigerator. Food that is allowed to come to room temperature can allow harmful bacteria to grow, which can cause illness. It takes longer to thaw food in the refrigerator, so some meals will need to be placed in the refrigerator to thaw the day before you plan to serve them. The larger, thicker and denser the frozen meal, the longer it will take to thaw. For example, frozen, uncooked chicken takes longer to thaw than cooked, shredded chicken in a recipe.

Ideally, you would remove a meal from the freezer the day before so that it has time to thaw by the time you need it. However, if there are days that your life is less than ideal and yesterday you weren't thinking about what is for dinner today - all is not lost!

Some meals can be thawed and heated in the microwave. However, you should never microwave food in a plastic bowl or bag, unless it is labeled **microwave safe**. I'm not a scientist but I have read articles that say that heating food in plastic, especially food that contains any fat, can overheat the plastic and cause toxins to be released into the food. You can't see, smell or taste the toxins but who knows? You could come down with some hideous ailment from toxins from overheated plastic! So, play it safe and remove the meal from the bag and place it in a microwave safe dish. Since the food does not pour when frozen you will need to tear or cut the sides of the bag so it can be easily removed.

Recipes with pasta in them should be allowed to thaw undisturbed. Forced thawing and any stirring can cause the pasta to get mushy and fall apart. Recipes with pasta should be handled as little as possible.

If the meal you have chosen for dinner is still frozen, you will need to add approximately 50% to the baking time. If it is in a freezer bag, remove the meal from the bag and place it in a dish. An easy way to remove a frozen meal from a freezer bag is to cut or tear the sides of the bag at the seam. Follow the instructions for the recipe but bake it for approximately 50% more than the recommended time. This is a *general* rule, not an exact science.

You can take the guess work out of determining if the meal is hot by using an *instant read thermometer*. These look similar to meat thermometers but you never leave this kind in the oven with the food. Insert the thermometer into the center of the meal and it will instantly tell you the temperature of the food. These thermometers come with a guide that lists the recommended temperature for different types of food, usually between 160 and 170. Both dial and digital read instant read thermometers are easy to find, usually with the kitchen gadgets.

Chapter 11

Sample Order of Events

✔ **Gather Equipment**

✔ **Choose Recipes**

Slow Cooker
Brown Sugar Pork Ribs, page 72
Cream Cheese Chicken, page 86

Oven
Oven Stew, page 102
Candied Chicken, page 111

StoveTop
Taco Soup, page 132
Chicken Tortellini Soup, page 135

Assemble
Spaghetti and Company, page 161
Cheese Manicotti, page 162
Simply Lasagna, page 164
Barbeque Beef and Biscuits, page 170
Meat Loaf and Potatoes, page 172
Tortilla Chicken, page 208
Ham and Chicken Roll-Ups, page 210
Cheesy Ham and Potatoes, page 217
Tuna Bow Ties, page 224

✔ **List Chosen Recipes**

✔ **Make Shopping List**

✔ Shop

✔ Arrange Recipe Cards

Place Slow Cooker recipe cards next to the slow cooker. Cream Cheese Chicken on top and then Brown Sugar Pork Ribs next. Always start the shortest cooking time recipe first with Slow Cooker recipes.

Place Oven recipe cards beside the oven. Since both will probably fit in the oven at the same time, it does not matter which recipe card comes first.

Place both StoveTop recipe cards beside the stove. Place Taco Soup on the top, then Chicken Tortellini Soup second. If you have cooked chicken and have chicken broth left, always make the chicken soup recipe last. You want to be able to use as much of the chicken broth as you need in other recipes. When you are sure you don't need any more broth, use the remainder to make chicken soup.

Arrange the Assemble recipe cards in the following order:
• Spaghetti and Company
• Cheese Manicotti
• Simply Lasagna
• Ham and Chicken Roll-Ups
• BBQ Beef and Biscuits
• Tuna Bow Ties
• Tortilla Chicken
• Meat Loaf and Potatoes
• Cheesy Ham and Potatoes

Place these recipe cards on the counter top or wherever you have chosen to Assemble your recipes. The order is not mandatory, but try assembling the most difficult or time con-suming recipes first, and save the easiest and quickest recipes for the end of your cooking day.

✔ **Make any "Day Before" preparations you have time for.**
- Arrange groceries for easy access.
- Get out any other needed items.
- Cook chicken for all recipes that call for cooked chicken.
- Chop onions for all recipes that call for chopped onion.
- Prepare any other needed vegetables.
- Shred cheese for all recipes that call for shredded cheese.

✔ **Cooking Day Order of Events**
1. If you did not cook the chicken the day before, put the chicken in large pot of salted water. Add 1 celery stalk, 1 carrot, 1 onion cut in half, and a few peppercorns. Boil slowly on a back burner until chicken is cooked through. When fully cooked, remove the chicken to cool but save the broth for **Chicken Tortellini Soup**. Meanwhile....

2. Start **Cream Cheese Chicken** in the slow cooker. Write down *what time it will be* when you need to remove chicken and add soup and cream cheese.

3. Chop the onions, if you did not chop them the day before.

4. Shred all the cheese if it is not already shredded and/or if you did not shred it the day before.

5. Put **Oven Stew** in the oven. Write down *what time* to remove it from the oven.

6. Put **Candied Chicken** in the oven. Write down *what time* to remove it from the oven.

7. Start **Taco Soup**. Write down *what time* it will be done.

8. Start rice in the rice cooker, if you have one. If you don't have a rice cooker, cook rice on the front burner of your stove. Use a timer.

9. If the chicken is cooked through, remove from heat, cool and chop or shred it into bowls.

10. Make the **Spaghetti Sauce**.

11. Don't forget about the **Taco Soup**. When it is done, set it aside to cool and start **Chicken Tortellini Soup**. Write down *what time* it will be done.

12. Don't forget about **Candied Chicken**. When it is done, remove it from oven and allow to cool.

13. Don't forget about **Cream Cheese Chicken**. When it is done, set it aside to cool and start **Brown Sugar Pork Ribs**. Write down *what time* to drain and add sauce.

14. Assemble **Manicotti**. Do NOT cook the pasta. Freeze.

15. Package and freeze any meals that have cooled completely.

16. Don't forget about **Oven Stew**. When it is done, set it aside to cool.

17. Don't forget about **Chicken Tortellini Soup**. When it is done, set it aside to cool.

18. Assemble **Lasagna**. Do NOT cook the pasta. Freeze.

19. Put remaining sauce in bags for **Spaghetti**. Freeze.

20. Assemble **Ham and Chicken Roll-Ups**. Freeze.

21. Cook Bow Tie pasta. Use a timer. When done, rinse with cold water.

22. While pasta is cooking, make **BBQ Beef and Biscuits**. Freeze.

23. Assemble **Tuna Bow Ties**. Freeze.

24. Don't forget about **Brown Sugar Pork Ribs**. Drain, add sauce and write down *what time* it will be done.

25. Assemble **Tortilla Chicken**. Freeze.

26. Package and freeze any meals that have cooled completely.

27. Assemble **Meatloaf and Potatoes**. Freeze.

28. Assemble **Cheesy Ham and Potatoes**. Freeze.

29. Package and freeze any remaining meals that have cooled completely.

29. Bag and freeze any remaining (extra) rice.

30. When **Brown Sugar Pork Ribs** are done, allow to cool and freeze.

✔ **Admire your full freezer! Isn't it a beautiful thing?!**

Being prepared and organized, and utilizing multiple cooking methods at the same time is the most productive way to accomplish much in a short period of time.   However, preparing 30 meals in one day is certainly not an exact science.   This outline is only meant to be a *guideline*.   It is intended to show you what is going on at the same time and what comes next. The time it takes to do particular tasks will vary from recipe to recipe, from cook to cook.   Do not be discouraged if the process does not flow exactly as outlined.   Some things may take longer and others may advance more quickly for you.   This outline is intended to give you a *general* idea of the order of events.

Chapter 12

Other Options

There may be times that you desire to prepare meals for your freezer but you do not have the time or ability to devote an entire day to the process. Perhaps you have a tiny baby and you are lucky to get a shower in sometime during the day, let alone spend all day cooking. Maybe you have a very hectic work schedule and you cannot give up an entire day to cooking. Maybe you have health issues. Your back, your knees, your feet or other ailments won't allow you to stand all day in the kitchen. Perhaps you just don't want to prepare 30 meals in one day! There is no rule that says you *must* choose 15 recipes.

If you cannot or just don't want to prepare 15 recipes, try choosing 5 recipes. Prepare one recipe in the slow cooker, one in the oven, one on the stove top and assemble two at your kitchen counter. When you are finished you will have 10 meals in your freezer! Ten meals is a beautiful thing! Ten meals in your freezer is 10 days of freedom in your future. Freedom on the day the baby doesn't sleep all night, the day you have to work late, the day you have an unexpected meeting. You can still put a delicious meal on the table.

The number of meals you prepare is not important. Do whatever you can do. Prepare only two or three if you want. Even if you only have time to make dinner for that night, be sure to make enough for 2 meals. Put one on the table for dinner and package the other for the freezer. The important thing is that you put some meals in the freezer for the days you do not have time to cook.

To really make the most of your cooking experience, take advantage of sales as they come. Buying everything on the day before you cook leaves you at the mercy of the grocery store and you will pay whatever the price is that day, whether the food item is on sale or not.

When chicken goes on sale, buy the amount of chicken you think you will need for cooking day, freeze it and have it on hand for when you are ready to cook. Likewise, buy up ground beef and other meats that you prefer to cook as they are on sale and store them in your freezer until you are ready to cook.

Different sources will tell you that you cannot refreeze meat, because of the danger of the thawed meat coming to room temperature and allowing harmful bacteria to grow. Freezing does not kill the bacteria, it just postpones the day you get sick! You can refreeze meat as long as you never allow it to come to room temperature. Always thaw meat in the refrigerator and, preferably, use it while it still contains ice crystals.

While preparing 30 meals from 15 different recipes in one day provides a wide variety of meals, it is certainly not your only option. You could choose to cook just chicken recipes one week when chicken is on sale and then just ground beef recipes the next week when ground beef goes on sale. On one occasion our local grocery store had a great sale on boneless skinless chicken breasts. To get the great sale price I was required to purchase a case of 40 pounds of chicken! Rather than putting all the chicken in the freezer and then thawing part of it when cooking day came around, I prepared and froze only chicken recipes.

Another option is to prepare a *category* of recipes, such as recipes using spaghetti sauce. Whether you make your own, or you doctor the canned variety of spaghetti sauce, on one day make only recipes that use spaghetti sauce. Get your largest pan, perhaps it is your pressure canner, and prepare in it as much sauce as it will hold. Make as many recipes of Lasagna, Manicotti and any other recipes that call for spaghetti sauce, as you can and package as many containers of spaghetti sauce as you desire.

Another category is meatballs. You could prepare many recipes of meatballs and sauces. Whatever your recipe for meatballs, double or triple the recipe. Mix it well with your hands and spread it out on a clean counter top. Pat it flat about one-inch thick all over. Then, using a pizza cutter, gently cut the whole thing into one-inch squares. Be sure to use the type of pizza cutter with the large wheel cutter. The small ones are not deep enough to accommodate the thickness of the meatball.

Line cookie sheets with foil and spray the foil with non-stick cooking spray. The foil is very important for a speedy clean up. Pick up each square and give it a quick roll in the palms of your hands to shape it into a ball. Place the meatballs close together on the cookie sheet, but not touching. Bake them for about 7 minutes. You do not want to bake them fully since they will continue to cook in a sauce and/or when they are heated for serving. They then can be frozen in a single layer and placed as they are in freezer bags. They can be added to sauces, ready to be heated and served.

There may be times when you desire to eat something you do not have in the freezer. If the stars line up and this desire coincides with a day that you have time to cook, make double or triple of the desired recipe. Serve one and freeze the others.

Cooking with someone else can be a truly rewarding experience. Not only is it fun to be together, a lot more can be
accomplished with two or more sets of hands. Cooking with
a friend is great fun. Combine forces and cook for both of you
at once or cook in your kitchen for you and in her kitchen for
her.

Cooking with family members can also be a fabulous experience. Not only can you accomplish more with help but it can
be a valuable learning experience for kids.

Consider involving other family members in the heating and
serving process, too. If you are stuck in traffic or in a meeting that is running late, you can call home and have who ever
answers the phone choose dinner from the freezer, and follow the instructions that you have put on the package. Dinner can be ready by the time you get home! Coming home to
dinner ready and on the table is a beautiful thing!

Another option, especially if you have family members old
enough to help, is to assign each family member a day of the
week to be responsible for dinner. They can choose dinner
from the list of chosen recipes, follow the directions and
make it ready to eat. While it is heating they can prepare
any desired side dishes to serve with the meal.

Chapter 13

Blessing the Lives of Others

Now that you know how to freeze food for your family, you are armed with knowledge that can truly bless the lives of others.

Meals frozen in disposable foil pans are very convenient for taking a meal into a neighbor or loved one. When you have meals in your freezer, no matter how busy you are, you can always choose a meal, effortlessly make it hot and ready to eat, and take it to a friend or loved one in need. The disposable pan makes for zero cleanup for them. They do not have the burden of returning a dish to you and you never lose another dish. This is a beautiful thing!

Don't overlook the value of single servings. As you package each recipe, consider packaging single servings. These are handy to take to work for lunch and/or on days you don't want macaroni and cheese for lunch, again.

Single servings could also bless the lives of others. Perhaps you have an elderly parent, grandparent(s), elderly neighbors or other homebound loved ones. Whatever the situation, for those who have a difficult time preparing meals, consider how stocking their freezer could bless their lives. You could keep their freezer stocked with single servings or meals for two.

One option is to devote an entire cooking day to preparing meals packaged for one or two. There will be no need to double recipes since, generally, a recipe for 6 will make three meals for two people, and even more single servings.

Package the meals in small foil pans for one or two if it is a meal that is to be baked in the oven. Package all others in reusable plastic freezer containers. These can be easily microwaved, making for simple preparation for your loved one. If the meal is to be served with rice or pasta, place the rice or pasta in the container first and cover with the sauce or gravy, etc. This can also work with mashed potatoes if they are very thick.

Another option is to prepare meals for them at the same time that you freeze meals for your family. When you make your shopping list be sure to add an appropriate number of chicken pieces, etc. I have done this consistently for my husband's beloved grandmother. Every time I put meals in my freezer, I package two or three meals of each recipe for grandma. I place them all in a freezer basket in my chest freezer and then every other week or so I take some over and stack them in grandma's refrigerator freezer. This is helpful to her and keeps her from the painful task of standing for so long in the kitchen preparing meals for herself. It also spares her the expense and tedium of store bought frozen dinners.

A truly fun and beneficial option is to have a Baby Shower in which you make meals for the expectant mother. This is especially helpful to the mother who already has children. She probably already has baby booties and blankets. What she truly needs is meals in her freezer! This can be done different ways. One way is to freeze meals at home and each guest brings one or more meals for the expectant mother. Another option is to get together to make the meals. Everyone brings assigned items and you work together to cook and/or assemble the meals. The guest of honor goes home with the goods!

Chapter 14

Shortcuts

There are many time-saving shortcuts that can help you make the cooking and freezing process a smooth experience. As you prepare meals for the freezer, be alert to shortcuts that streamline the process and make it easier and time efficient. Make use of the following shortcuts that appeal to you, and add your own discoveries. Remember that there is not *one* specific way to prepare 30 meals in one day. These are guidelines. Make your own rules and change the process to fit your style and circumstances. Do not be a slave to directions.

✂ If you have cooked chicken for several recipes, divide the chicken into a bowl for each meal. Place the recipe card in front of the bowl and continue to add ingredients until that recipe is complete. Remember you will be cooking your chicken all at once for all the recipes that call for cooked chicken. Then you will be chopping or shredding the chicken. If you have three recipes that call for cooked, chopped chicken, divide your chicken among three bowls, rather than taking out chicken one recipe at a time and leaving to chance how much chicken you will actually have left for that last recipe. If you have many recipes that call for cooked chicken, divide the chicken in half. Leave one half in a large bowl, divide the other half among the three or four bowls.

✂ When making favorite recipes such as spaghetti sauce, chili and taco soup, consider making as much as your pan will hold and divide it into family-sized portions for the freezer. Do you find it frustrating to spend hours making your favorite spaghetti sauce, only to have it consumed in six and a half minutes? Depending on your family size you may want to make more than double of a recipe. A huge pan of your favorite meal doesn't take much more time to prepare than a single meal of your favorite recipe. Make as much as your pan will hold and package it for the freezer in meal-sized portions. You'll get six and a half minutes of pleasure many times over!

✂ When you purchase foil baking pans, buy the sizes you *really* need for your family. I used to make my lasagna in a 9 x 13-inch pan. My family would eat about half of it and the remainder would go into the refrigerator for that obligatory 3 days until the disposal or the dog got the rest of it. Perhaps we would eat leftovers another day but we would almost never consume an entire 9 x 13-inch pan of lasagna. I have discovered that a 9 x 9-inch pan of lasagna is plenty for my family. Decide what size your family needs, decide if you desire leftovers and plan accordingly.

✂ On cooking day, spread out all the disposable foil pans that you will be filling. Spray each pan with non-stick cooking spray. Now all your pans are ready to be filled and you won't have to repeatedly pick up and spray each pan as you go. You will also never again forget to spray a pan!

✂ If you prefer to use labels, make them the day before you need them. Print them out using the **30 Meals in One Day** computer program. Or tear or cut off strips of masking tape and stick them to the back of a cookie sheet(s). Write out your labels with name and cooking instructions. Place the labels on the table or wherever you choose to package your meals for the freezer. As each meal is packaged you can choose the appropriate label and attach it.

✂ Tape your List of Chosen Recipes (Menu) that you have prepared and placed in your freezer, on the door of the freezer, on the inside of a cupboard door or some other convenient place where you can refer to it often and keep it updated. This way, not only will you have a "menu," but you will also always know what you have in your freezer.

✂ There are some Oven recipes that can be baked then packaged for the freezer OR they can be frozen prior to baking. If you bake a meal then freeze it, you can simply thaw and heat in the microwave. If you freeze the uncooked meal such as chicken and sauce, you will thaw and pour it into a baking dish, and bake it on the day you are going to serve it. Each method has its advantages. One is ready in a hurry. One makes the house smell delicious while it's baking.

✂ Some recipes that call for marinating beef, pork, turkey or chicken can be marinated in the freezer. Simply prepare the marinade, pour it over the meat and freeze it in a freezer bag. After it is thawed, the marinating will be complete. Ready to cook!

✂ Do you have occasions in your life that take three hours or so? Most frozen meals can be baked for about three hours at 300° and come out hot and delicious. Cover the dinner with foil and place the frozen dinner in the oven. Program your oven to bake for three hours at 300° and go to the baseball game! This is also great for Sunday morning. Put a frozen meal in the oven before you leave and when you get home, Dinner is Ready! **Chicken and Rice** is one exception to this because frozen raw chicken is dense and takes longer to thaw. This recipe will not be done after only three hours at 300° when you start it in the frozen state.

✄ Try freezing a few extra recipes in pans that don't really *need* to be in pans. You will enjoy the convenience of putting one in the oven - even when frozen solid - programming your oven to bake it, and then coming home to a piping hot dinner. This is helpful on days when you are not going to be available to pour the thawed meal into a baking dish to bake. For example, freeze **Sweet and Sour Chicken** in a disposable foil baking pan. On your way out the door, toss it in the oven and put some rice in the rice cooker. You can come home to the house smelling lovely and you can say Dinner is Ready!

✄ When mincing fresh garlic use a metal garlic press. The plastic type can break. Even easier and almost as good as fresh garlic is the bottled minced garlic that you can get in the produce section at the grocery store. It is in a small bottle next to the fresh garlic and is usually very inexpensive. The same is true for ginger.

✄ If you want to prepare a recipe that calls for ham and you don't want to purchase a whole or half ham, just get what you need from the delicatessen at the grocery store. Ask the deli to cut an inch thick slice or two of ham. Deli ham is also great when a recipe calls for a few slices of ham.

✄ When making enchiladas, consider tearing the tortillas and making layers instead of rolling each enchilada. The meal goes together faster and gets eaten just as fast as the rolled enchiladas!

✄ There is no need to cook lasagna noodles when you are going to freeze them prior to baking. The noodles absorb moisture during freezing, thawing and baking. They soften up beautifully and taste delicious. Just break them to fit whatever size pan you have chosen and use them in your regular lasagna recipes.

✂ There is no need to cook manicotti noodles when you are going to freeze them. They are easier to fill uncooked, too! When filling manicotti tubes, place the filling in a small resealable freezer bag. Cut the corner off the bag, fit the opening into one end of the manicotti tube, and squeeze the filling into each one. Do not use regular resealable sandwich bags since the seams are more fragile and they may burst as you apply pressure to the bag. Place filled manicotti on a bed of sauce. Leave a finger width space between each manicotti to allow it room to expand as it absorbs moisture. Cover completely with sauce so the pasta has a source of moisture.

✂ If you top a meal with cheese and then cover it with foil, the cheese can stick to the foil when you uncover it after it is baked. For a recipe that calls for a top layer of shredded cheese, such as lasagna, you can rearrange the layers, so that the cheese does not come last. Put the last layer of cheese next to last and top with a layer of sauce instead. When you serve the meal you can add a light sprinkling of cheese to make it beautiful.

✂ If your recipe calls for a topping of shredded cheese, crumbs or French fried onions, you shouldn't freeze them on the food since they absorb moisture and can get soggy. However, you can place the shredded cheese, crumbs or onions in a small zipper freezer bag and place it in the freezer bag with the food or tape it to the foil baking pan. You'll have it at your fingertips exactly when you need it.

✂ If you have spaghetti sauce left after preparing your favorite Italian recipes, place the remaining spaghetti sauce in a small freezer bag to make pizza. Usually a cup or two is all you will need for each pizza.

✂ If you are going to be gone for at least an hour, you can have potatoes ready to mash right when you get home. Before you leave, bring a pot of cubed potatoes to a full boil. Turn off the heat, but leave it on the burner with the lid on. The potatoes will be ready for mashing when you return.

✂ For perfect rice every time, even when you are not home, measure rice and water into a pan. Bring to a boil. Turn off the heat, but leave the pan on the burner with the lid on. The rice will be fluffy and perfect in about an hour.

Use the shortcuts listed here that you find convenient. As you continue to freeze meals, you are sure to discover your own shortcuts that make your cooking experience more convenient and more enjoyable. Whatever method you settle on or whatever the number of recipes you decide to make, enjoy the journey! May your freezer always be full!

Chapter 15

Recipe Section

Slow Cooker Recipes . . . . .pages 70 - 99

Oven Recipes . . . . .pages 100 - 117

StoveTop Recipes . . . . .pages 118 - 154

Assemble Recipes . . . . .pages 155 - 228

Slow Cooker Recipes

Beef Stroganoff, 80
Brown Sugar Pork Ribs, 72
Chicken Cacciatore, 88
Chicken with Mushroom Gravy, 87
Continental Chicken, 89
Corned Beef and Cabbage, 82
Country Barbequed Ribs, 85
Crab, Shrimp, or Lobster Newberg, 90
Cream Cheese Chicken, 86
French Onion Soup, 99
Grandma's Beef Stew, 79
Honey Barbequed Ribs, 71
Italian Meat Sauce, 95
Italian Roast, 83
Manhattan Clam Chowder, 92
Minestrone, 98
New England Baked Beans, 93
New England Clam Chowder, 91
Old Fashioned Bean Soup, 94
Polynesian Pork Roast, 75
Slow Cooked Short Ribs, 77
Slow Cooked Chili, 97
Slow Cooked Goulash, 78
Slow Cooked Stew, 76
Slow Cooked Stroganoff, 76
Smothered Steak, 84
Swedish Meatballs, 81
Swiss Steak and Gravy, 73
Tomato Swiss Steak, 74
Vegetable Beef Soup, 96

Honey Barbequed Ribs

3 pounds boneless pork ribs
1/2 teaspoon garlic salt
1/2 teaspoon pepper
1 cup ketchup
1/2 cup brown sugar
1/2 cup honey
1/4 cup spicy brown mustard
2 tablespoons Worcestershire sauce
1 1/2 teaspoons liquid smoke

Place pork ribs in the bottom of slow cooker. Cover and cook on High for 3 hours. Drain and discard liquid. Reduce heat to Low. In a bowl, combine garlic salt, pepper, ketchup, brown sugar, honey, spicy brown mustard, Worcestershire sauce and liquid smoke. Mix well. Pour over ribs in slow cooker. Cover and cook on Low for 3 hours. Remove from slow cooker and allow to cool. Place in freezer bag. Label and freeze. 8 servings.

To serve: Thaw. Heat until hot throughout.

Brown Sugar Pork Ribs

3 pounds boneless pork ribs
1 cup chopped onion
2 teaspoons minced garlic
3 tablespoons butter
2 tablespoons soy sauce
3/4 cup lemon juice
1 teaspoon salt
1/2 teaspoon pepper
2 cups brown sugar

Place ribs in slow cooker. Cover and cook on High for 3 hours. Drain and discard liquid. In a small skillet, cook onion and garlic in butter until soft. Add soy sauce, lemon juice, salt, pepper and brown sugar. Cook and stir until sugar is dissolved. Pour over ribs. Cover and cook on High for 2 hours. Remove from slow cooker. Allow to cool. Place in freezer bag. Label and freeze. 8 servings.

To serve: Thaw. Heat until hot throughout. Serve with rice.

To juice a lemon quickly, easily and thoroughly, place a lemon in a glass bowl in the microwave. Heat until the lemon bursts (approximately 1 minute, depending on the size of the lemon.) Turn off microwave as soon as the lemon bursts. Allow to cool for a few minutes. The lemon juice can then be easily squeezed from the hole made by the escaping steam.

Swiss Steak and Gravy

3 tablespoons flour
1/4 teaspoon garlic salt
1/4 teaspoon onion salt
1/4 teaspoon pepper
2 pounds beef round steak
3 tablespoons canola oil
2 cups sliced onions
1 1/2 cups beef broth
1 tablespoon sugar
2 tablespoons Worcestershire sauce
1 cup beef broth
1/4 cup flour
1/4 teaspoon salt
1/8 teaspoon pepper

Combine 3 tablespoons flour, garlic salt, onion salt and pepper. Mix well. Coat steak with the flour mixture. Pound with a meat mallet. Turn meat over and continue to pound in as much flour as the meat will hold. Brown steak on all sides in 3 tablespoons hot oil. Layer browned steak and sliced onions in a slow cooker. Mix 1 1/2 cups beef broth, sugar and Worcestershire. Pour over all. Cover, cook on High for 4 hours. Remove steak to cool. Whisk 1/4 cup flour into 1 cup beef broth. Add salt and pepper. Pour into slow cooker and mix well. Heat to boil and stir until thick and bubbly. Remove gravy and allow to cool. Put steak and gravy into freezer bag. Label and freeze. 8 servings.

To serve: Thaw. Heat in until hot and bubbly. Serve gravy over hot mashed potatoes.

Tomato Swiss Steak

2 pounds beef round steak
1/2 teaspoon salt
1/8 teaspoon pepper
2 cups sliced onion
2 cups baby carrots
1 (10.75-ounce) can beefy mushroom soup
1 (8-ounce) can tomato sauce
1 tablespoon sugar

Cut steak into serving-sized pieces. Sprinkle with salt and pepper. Place steaks in slow cooker and cover with sliced onions. Place baby carrots over beef and onions. Combine soup, tomato sauce and sugar. Pour over carrots in slow cooker. Cover and cook on Low for 6 to 8 hours or on High for 4 hours. Remove from slow cooker and allow to cool. Place in freezer bag. Label and freeze. 8 servings.

To serve: Thaw. Heat until steaks are hot throughout and gravy is hot and bubbly. Serve over rice, noodles or potatoes.

Polynesian Pork Roast

1 (4 pound) pork roast
3/4 cup pineapple apricot jam
1/2 cup brown sugar
1 teaspoon minced garlic
1/4 cup apple cider vinegar
1/2 cup soy sauce
1/4 cup molasses
2 cups chicken broth

Place pork roast in slow cooker. Combine preserves, brown sugar, garlic, vinegar, soy sauce, molasses and chicken broth. Mix well. Pour over roast. Cover and cook on Low for 8 hours. Remove roast and sauce from slow cooker. Allow to cool. Place cooled roast and sauce in freezer bag. Label and freeze. 12 servings.

To serve: Thaw. Heat roast and sauce until hot and bubbly. Pull roast into serving pieces (or shred) and serve sauce over rice.

To thicken sauce, heat sauce to boiling in a small saucepan. Dissolve 2 tablespoons cornstarch in 1/4 cup water. Stir into sauce. Cook and stir until sauce is thick and glossy. Sauce may be thickened before or after freezing.

Slow Cooked Stew

2 pounds beef stew meat
2 (10.75-ounce) cans cream of mushroom soup
1 (1.25-ounce) envelope onion soup mix
1/2 cup water

Cut beef stew meat into 1-inch cubes. Place stew meat into slow cooker. Mix soup, soup mix and water until smooth. Pour over stew meat in slow cooker. Cover and cook on High for 4 hours. Remove from slow cooker and allow to cool. Place in freezer bag or container. Label and freeze. 8 servings.

To serve: Thaw. Heat until hot and bubbly. Serve over mashed potatoes, rice, or hot buttered noodles.

For delicious **Slow Cooked Stew**, cook 3/4 cup sliced mushrooms in 2 tablespoons butter until lightly browned and limp. Add to thawed Slow Cooked Stew. Heat until bubbly. Remove from heat and add 1 cup sour cream. Serve over hot buttered noodles.

Slow Cooked Short Ribs

2/3 cups flour
2 teaspoons salt
1/2 teaspoon pepper
4 pounds boneless beef short ribs
1/3 cup butter
1 1/2 cups beef broth
1 cup chopped onion
3/4 cup brown sugar
3/4 cup apple cider vinegar
1/2 cup ketchup
3 tablespoons Worcestershire sauce
1/2 cup chili sauce
2 teaspoons minced garlic
1 1/2 teaspoon chili powder
1/2 cup corn syrup

Combine flour, salt and pepper. Coat ribs with flour mixture. In a large skillet, brown ribs on all sides in butter. Transfer browned ribs to slow cooker. In same skillet, combine beef broth, onion, brown sugar, vinegar, ketchup, Worcestershire sauce, chili sauce, garlic, chili powder and corn syrup. Mix well. Heat until mixture comes to a boil. Pour over ribs in slow cooker. Cover and cook on Low for 9 to 10 hours. Remove from slow cooker and allow to cool. Place in freezer bag. Label and freeze. 12 servings.

To serve: Thaw. Heat until hot and bubbly.

Slow Cooked Goulash

2 pounds beef stew meat
1 cup chopped onion
1 teaspoon minced garlic
2 tablespoons flour
1 teaspoon salt
1/2 teaspoon pepper
1 1/2 teaspoons paprika
1 (14.5-ounces) can diced tomatoes
1 cup sour cream

Cut beef stew meat into 1-inch cubes. Place stew meat, onion and garlic in slow cooker. Stir together flour, salt, pepper and paprika. Add to slow cooker and stir to coat meat. Stir in the tomatoes. Cover and cook on High for 4 to 5 hours. Add sour cream. Remove from slow cooker and allow to cool. Place in freezer bag. Label and freeze. 8 servings.

To serve: Thaw. Heat until hot and bubbly. Serve over hot, buttered noodles.

Grandma's Beef Stew

2 pounds beef stew meat
3 cups sliced carrots
1 cup chopped onion
1 cup sliced celery
2 (14.5-ounces) cans stewed tomatoes
1/2 cup quick cooking tapioca
1 whole clove
2 bay leaves
1 teaspoon salt
1/2 teaspoon pepper

Cut beef stew meat into 1-inch cubes. Place stew meat in slow cooker. Add carrots, onion, celery and tomatoes. Stir in tapioca, clove, bay leaves, salt and pepper. Cover and cook on Low for 10 to 12 hours or High for 5 to 6 hours. Remove from slow cooker and allow to cool. Remove clove and bay leaves. Place in freezer bag. Label and freeze. 8 servings.

To serve: Thaw. Heat until hot and bubbly. Serve with cornbread or sourdough bread.

Beef Stroganoff

2 pounds beef stew meat
3/4 cup sliced fresh mushrooms
1 (1.25-ounces) envelope onion soup mix
1 (10.75-ounces) can cream of mushroom soup
3 tablespoons red wine vinegar
1/4 cup quick cooking tapioca
1 cup sour cream

Cut beef stew meat into 1-inch cubes. Place stew meat and mushrooms in slow cooker. Combine soup mix, soup and vinegar. Stir in tapioca. Cover and cook on Low for 8 to 12 hours or on High for 4 to 6 hours. Stir in sour cream. Remove from slow cooker and allow to cool. Place in freezer bag. Label and freeze. 8 servings.

To serve: Thaw. Heat and stir until smooth and hot throughout. Serve over hot, buttered noodles.

Swedish Meatballs

2 pounds lean ground beef
1/4 cup corn flake crumbs
1/4 cup minced onion
2 eggs, slightly beaten
1 teaspoon celery salt
1/2 teaspoon garlic powder
1 cup sliced mushrooms
2 (10.75-ounces) cans cream of mushroom soup
1/2 cup evaporated milk
1 tablespoon Worcestershire sauce

Mix ground beef, corn flake crumbs, onion, eggs, celery salt and garlic powder. Mix well and shape into 1-inch balls. Brown on all sides in hot skillet or bake on foil-lined baking sheet for 7 minutes at 350°. Place meatballs and mushrooms in slow cooker. Mix soup, milk and Worcestershire sauce. Pour over meatballs. Cover and cook on High for 1 hour. Stir. Reduce heat to Low and cook for 3 hours. Remove from slow cooker and allow to cool. Place in freezer bag. Label and freeze. 8 servings.

To serve: Thaw. Heat until sauce is smooth, hot and bubbly and meatballs are hot throughout. Serve over hot buttered noodles.

To easily make cornflake crumbs, place corn flakes in a zippered plastic bag. Place bag on a flat surface. Roll a rolling pin over the flakes until crushed to the desired size.

Corned Beef and Cabbage

1 (3 pound) corned beef brisket
1 1/2 cups sliced carrots
2 cups quartered onions
1 cup water
3 cups cabbage wedges

Place corned beef brisket, carrots, onion and water in slow cooker. Cover and cook on High for 5 to 6 hours. Add cabbage wedges. Push them down into the liquid. Cook on High for an additional 2 to 3 hours. Remove the brisket, cabbage and broth and allow to cool. Pull meat into chunks, if desired. Place in freezer bag. Label and freeze. 8 servings.

To serve: Thaw. Heat and serve.

If the corned beef brisket is too large to allow the amount of cabbage you desire, prepare additional cabbage separately in a skillet. Remove 1 cup broth from the slow cooker during the last hour of cooking. Pour over cabbage wedges in skillet. Cover and cook slowly for 20 to 30 minutes.

Italian Roast

1 (4 pound) beef roast
1 teaspoon salt
1 teaspoon minced garlic
1 cup sliced mushrooms
1 cup chopped onion
1 (1.25-ounce) envelope spaghetti sauce mix
1 (8-ounce) can tomato sauce
2 tablespoons butter
2 tablespoon flour

Season roast with salt. Place in slow cooker. Add garlic, mushrooms and onion. Combine spaghetti sauce mix and tomato sauce. Pour over roast and vegetables. Cover and cook on Low for 10 to 12 hours or on High for 6 hours. Remove from slow cooker. Melt butter in sauce pan. Stir in flour. Cook and stir over medium heat until bubbly. Add sauce. Cook until thick and bubbly. Add sliced or shredded roast. Allow to cool. Place in freezer bag. Label and freeze. 12 servings.

To serve: Heat through. Serve over hot pasta.

Smothered Steak

3 cups thin sliced onion
1/4 cup flour
1 teaspoon salt
1/4 teaspoon pepper
1/4 teaspoon paprika
1 1/2 pounds beef round steak
1 cup sliced mushrooms
1/2 cup beef broth
2 teaspoons Worcestershire sauce
2 tablespoons flour
3 tablespoons water

Place one cup sliced onion in bottom of slow cooker. Combine flour, salt, pepper and paprika. Cut steak into serving-sized pieces and coat in flour mixture. Place half of the steak pieces on top of the onions in the slow cooker. Add another cup sliced onion and the mushrooms. Top with remaining meat and sliced onion. Mix beef broth and Worcestershire sauce. Pour over all. Cover. Cook on Low for 8 to 10 hours. Remove steaks from slow cooker. Whisk 2 tablespoons flour into 3 tablespoons water. Stir into slow cooker. cook until thick and bubbly. Remove from slow cooker and allow to cool. Place steaks and sauce in freezer bag. Label and freeze. 6 servings.

To serve: Thaw. Heat and stir until gravy is smooth and hot, and steaks are heated through.

Country Barbequed Ribs

3 pounds boneless pork ribs
1 teaspoon salt
1/8 teaspoon pepper
2 cups barbeque sauce

Place ribs in slow cooker. Sprinkle with salt and pepper. Cover and cook on High for 4 to 6 hours or on Low for 8 to 10 hours. Remove ribs from slow cooker and allow to cool. Discard liquid. Place ribs in freezer bag. Cover with barbeque sauce. Label and freeze. 8 servings.

To serve: Thaw. Heat in microwave or on stove top until hot and bubbly. Serve with baked potatoes.

These ribs will be fall-apart tender. The barbeque sauce may be added at the beginning but the sauce will be thin from the meat juices.

Cream Cheese Chicken

1 (.7-ounce) envelope Italian dressing mix
1/2 cup butter
2 pounds boneless skinless chicken breast
1 (10.75-ounce) can cream of chicken soup
1 (8-ounce) package cream cheese

Turn slow cooker on High. Melt butter in bottom of slow cooker. Stir Italian dressing mix into butter until well mixed. Cut chicken breasts into 1-inch strips. Place in slow cooker and stir to coat with butter and dressing mix. Cover and cook on High for 2 hours. Remove chicken to plate to cool. Add cream of chicken soup and cream cheese to the liquid in slow cooker. Stir to melt and mix until smooth and creamy. Remove sauce from slow cooker and allow to cool. Place chicken and sauce into freezer bag. Label and freeze. 6 servings.

To serve: Thaw. Heat and stir until smooth, hot and bubbly. Serve over mashed potatoes, rice, or hot buttered noodles.

Chicken with Mushroom Gravy

2 pounds boneless skinless chicken breast
1 teaspoon salt
1/4 teaspoon pepper
1 1/2 cups sliced mushrooms
1/4 cup chicken broth
1 (10.75-ounce) can cream of mushroom soup
1 cup sour cream
1/4 cup flour

Place chicken in slow cooker. Sprinkle with salt and pepper. Add mushrooms. Mix broth and soup. Pour over chicken. Cover and cook on Low for 7 to 9 hours or on High for 3 to 4 hours. Remove chicken from slow cooker and allow to cool. Shred chicken or pull into chunks, if desired. Stir together flour and sour cream. Stir into sauce. Allow to cool. Place chicken and sauce in freezer bag. Label and freeze. 6 servings.

To serve: Thaw. Heat and stir until smooth, thick and bubbly. Serve over rice, hot buttered noodles, or hot mashed potatoes.

Chicken Cacciatore

2 pounds boneless skinless chicken breast
1 cup chopped onion
1 1/2 cups sliced mushrooms
1 teaspoon salt
1/4 teaspoon pepper
2 (6-ounce) cans tomato paste
1 teaspoon minced garlic
1 teaspoon oregano
1/2 teaspoon basil
1/2 teaspoon celery seed
1 bay leaf
1/4 cup chicken broth

Cut chicken into serving-sized pieces. Place chicken, onion, mushrooms, salt and pepper in slow cooker. Combine tomato paste, garlic, oregano, basil, celery seed, bay leaf and chicken broth. Pour over chicken. Cover and cook on Low for 7 to 9 hours or on High for 3 to 4 hours. Remove bay leaf. Allow to cool. Place in freezer bag. Label and freeze. 6 servings.

To serve: Thaw. Heat until bubbly. Serve over hot pasta.

Continental Chicken

1 (2.5-ounce) envelope pressed, sliced beef
2 pounds boneless skinless chicken breast
6 slices bacon
1 (10.75-ounce) can cream of mushroom soup
1/4 cup sour cream
1/4 cup flour

Arrange beef slices on bottom of slow cooker. Partially cook bacon until beginning to brown but still soft. Wrap chicken with bacon and place on top of beef in slow cooker. Mix soup, sour cream and flour and pour over the chicken. Cover and cook on Low for 7 to 9 hours or on High for 3 to 4 hours. Remove from slow cooker and allow to cool. Place in freezer bag. Label and freeze. 6 servings.

To serve: Thaw. Heat and stir until smooth, hot and bubbly. Serve over hot buttered noodles or mashed potatoes.

Crab, Shrimp or Lobster Newberg

1/2 pound cooked crab, shrimp or lobster, chopped
1 (10.75-ounce) can cream of shrimp soup
3/4 cup evaporated milk
1 1/2 cups sliced mushrooms
2 egg yolks, beaten

Place crab, shrimp or lobster in slow cooker. Combine soup, milk and mushrooms and stir into slow cooker. Cover and cook on Low for 4 to 6 hours. Remove from slow cooker. Stir in egg yolks and allow to cool. Place in gallon freezer bag. Label and freeze. 4 servings.

To serve: Thaw. Heat and stir until smooth, hot and bubbly. Serve over hot rice and chow mein noodles or in puff pastry shells.

 Substitute cream of mushroom soup for the cream of shrimp soup, if desired.

New England Clam Chowder

3 (7-ounce) cans chopped clams
3 slices bacon, diced
1 cup chopped onion
1/2 cup sliced green onion
2 cups diced potatoes
1 1/2 cups water
1 1/2 teaspoons salt
1/4 teaspoon pepper
1 (12-ounce) can evaporated milk
1 (10.75-ounce) can cream of chicken soup
1 (10.75-ounce) can cream of celery soup

Place clams with their liquid in slow cooker. In skillet, cook and stir bacon and onion until golden and place in slow cooker. Add green onion and potatoes. Combine water, salt, pepper, evaporated milk and soups. Stir into slow cooker. Cover and cook on Low for 6 to 9 hours or on High for 4 hours. Remove from slow cooker and allow to cool. Place in freezer bag. Label and freeze. 6 servings.

To serve: Heat until hot and bubbly.

To easily slice green onions, peel off outside layer of onions. Cut off root ends. Holding several onions in one hand, use scissors (the longer the blades the better) to cut them all at once.

Manhattan Clam Chowder

3 (7-ounce) cans chopped clams
6 slices bacon, diced
1 cup chopped onion
1 cup sliced carrots
1 cup sliced celery
2 cups diced potato
1 tablespoon dried parsley flakes
1 teaspoon salt
2 whole peppercorns
1 bay leaf
1 teaspoon thyme
2 (14.5-ounce) cans stewed tomatoes

Place clams with their liquid in slow cooker. In a skillet, cook bacon and onion until onion is soft and bacon is starting to brown. Place in slow cooker. Add carrots, celery, potato, parsley, salt, peppercorns, bay leaf, thyme and tomatoes. Stir well. Cover and cook on Low for 8 hours or on High for 4 hours. Remove from slow cooker and allow to cool. Remove bay leaf and pepper-corns. Place in freezer bag. Label and freeze. 6 servings.

To serve: Thaw. Heat until hot and bubbly.

New England Baked Beans

3 cups dry Navy beans
1 pound smoked ham
1 cup chopped onion
1/2 cup packed brown sugar
1/2 cup maple syrup
1 teaspoon salt
1 teaspoon ground mustard
1 cup water
2/3 cup ketchup (optional)
2 tablespoons mustard (optional)

Cover beans with water and soak overnight. Drain and discard water. Cover beans with water again and boil for 10 minutes. Drain and discard water. Add beans to slow cooker. Add 1 cup water. Cut ham into cubes and add to slow cooker. Add onion. Combine brown sugar, maple syrup, salt, ground mustard and water. Add to slow cooker and mix well. Cover and cook on Low for 10 to 12 hours or on High for 4 to 5 hours. Stir in ketchup and mustard, if desired. Remove from slow cooker and allow to cool. Place in freezer bag. Label and freeze. 10 servings.

To serve: Thaw. Heat until hot and bubbly.

To use a meaty ham bone, place bone and all in slow cooker with beans. After cooling, trim ham from bone and add ham to beans before freezing.

Old Fashioned Bean Soup

2 cups dry Navy beans
1 pound smoked ham
1 teaspoon salt
3 whole peppercorns
2/3 cup chopped celery
1 cup chopped onion
1 bay leaf
2 quarts water

Cover beans with water and soak overnight. Drain and discard water. Cover with water again and boil for 10 minutes. Drain and discard water. Place beans in slow cooker. Cut ham into cubes. Add ham, salt, peppercorns, celery, onion, bay leaf and water to slow cooker. Mix well. Cover and cook on Low for 10 hours or on High for 6 hours. Remove from slow cooker and allow to cool. Remove bay leaf and peppercorns. Place in freezer bag. Label and freeze. 8 servings.

To serve: Thaw. Heat until hot and bubbly. Serve with corn bread and honey butter.

To use a meaty ham bone, place bone and all in slow cooker with beans. After cooling, trim ham from bone and add ham to beans before freezing.

Italian Meat Sauce

2 pounds ground beef
2 cups chopped onion
2 teaspoons minced garlic
1 (29-ounce) can tomato sauce
2 (6-ounce) cans tomato paste
2/3 cup chopped celery
2 teaspoons salt
1/2 teaspoon pepper
2 teaspoons oregano
1/4 teaspoon thyme
1 bay leaf

Brown ground beef with onions. Place in slow cooker. Combine garlic, tomato sauce, tomato paste, celery, salt, pepper, oregano, thyme and bay leaf. Add to slow cooker and mix well. Cover and cook on Low 12 hours or High 5 hours. Remove from slow cooker and allow to cool. Remove bay leaf. Place in freezer bag or use in recipes. Label and freeze. 10 servings.

To serve: Thaw. Heat until hot and bubbly. Serve over hot spaghetti. Top with Parmesan cheese.

 This sauce makes excellent lasagna, ravioli, manicotti and pizza!

Vegetable Beef Soup

1 pound beef stew meat
1 (14.5-ounce) can stewed tomatoes
1 cup sliced carrots
1 cup sliced celery
2 cups chopped onion
3 cups water
1 teaspoon salt
4 whole peppercorns
3 beef bouillon cubes
1 (10-ounce) package frozen mixed vegetables

Cut beef stew meat into 1-inch cubes. Place stew meat in slow cooker. Add tomatoes, carrots, celery and onion. Combine water, salt, peppercorns and bouillon cubes. Pour over meat and vegetables in slow cooker. Mix well. Cover and cook on Low for 10 hours or on High for 5 hours. Add thawed mixed vegetables during last hour of cooking. Remove from slow cooker and allow to cool. Remove peppercorns. Place in freezer bag. Label and freeze. 8 servings.

To serve: Thaw. Heat until hot and bubbly. Serve with crusty French bread.

Slow Cooked Chili

1 cup dry pinto beans
2 pounds ground beef
2 cups chopped onion
2 (14.5-ounce) cans stewed tomatoes
1 cup chopped green bell pepper
1/2 cup chopped celery
2 teaspoons minced garlic
2 tablespoons chili powder
1 teaspoon pepper
1 teaspoon cumin
2 tablespoons sugar
1 1/2 teaspoons salt

Cover beans with water and soak over night. Drain and discard water. Cover with water again and boil for 10 minutes. Drain and discard water. Place beans in slow cooker. Brown ground beef with onions. Add to slow cooker. Add tomatoes, green pepper, celery, garlic, chili powder, pepper, cumin, sugar and salt to slow cooker and mix well. Cover and cook on Low for 10 hours or on High for 5 hours. Remove from slow cooker and allow to cool. Place in freezer bag. Label and freeze. 8 servings.

To serve: Thaw. Heat until hot and bubbly. Serve with corn bread or crackers. Delicious topped with sour cream and shredded cheese.

 Substitute 2 (15-ounce) cans pinto beans for the 1 cup of dry pinto beans.

Minestrone

3 cups water
1 pound beef stew meat
1 cup chopped onion
1 cup sliced carrots
1 cup sliced celery
1 (4.5-ounce) Italian tomatoes
2 teaspoons salt
1/2 cup shredded cabbage
1 tablespoon basil
1 teaspoon minced garlic
1 teaspoon oregano
1/2 cup vermicelli
1 (16-ounce) can garbanzo beans
1 (10-ounce) package frozen mixed vegetables
1 cup sliced zucchini

Cut beef stew meat into 1-inch cubes. Place water and stew meat in slow cooker. Add onion, carrots, celery, tomatoes, salt, cabbage, basil, garlic, oregano, vermicelli and undrained beans. Cover and cook on Low for 10 hours or on High for 5 hours. Add thawed mixed vegetables and zucchini during last hour of cooking. Remove from slow cooker and allow to cool. Place in freezer bag. Label and freeze. 8 servings.

To serve: Thaw. Heat until hot and bubbly. Top with Parmesan cheese.

 Substitute any small pasta for the vermicelli.

French Onion Soup

3 cups thin sliced yellow onions
3 tablespoons butter
1 teaspoon salt
1 tablespoon sugar
2 tablespoons flour
4 cups beef broth
1 cup shredded fresh Parmesan cheese

Place onions and butter in large skillet. Cover and cook slowly for about 15 minutes. Uncover and add salt, sugar and flour. Mix well. Place in slow cooker with beef broth. Cover and cook on Low for 6 hours or on High for 3 hours. Remove from slow cooker and allow to cool. (Do not top with cheese until serving.) Place in freezer container. Label and freeze. 6 servings.

To serve: Thaw. Heat until hot and bubbly. Top with fresh Parmesan cheese. Serve with thick slices of French bread.

Oven Recipes

Bacon Chicken, 108
Baked Chicken in Gravy, 110
Calico Beans, 107
Candied Chicken, 111
Chicken Cordon Bleu, 117
Cornflake Chicken, 116
Country Style Barbeque Ribs, 101
Cranberry Chicken, 112
Hawaiian Chicken, 113
Meatballs in Gravy, 106
Oven Stew, 102
Peachy Chicken, 109
Pineapple Meatballs, 105
Porcupine Meatballs, 104
Smoky Maple Chicken, 115
Teriyaki Chicken, 114
Tomato Beef Stew, 103

Country Style Barbeque Ribs

3 pounds boneless pork ribs
1 1/2 cups barbeque sauce

Seal ribs tightly in extra heavy foil and place in baking pan. Bake at 325° for at least 3 hours. Remove from oven and allow to cool. Drain and discard liquid. Place ribs in freezer bag. Cover with barbeque sauce. Label and freeze. 12 servings.

To serve: Thaw. Heat through.

Consider baking enough ribs for several meals at the same time. Place cooled ribs in a separate bag for each meal. Cover each with a different sauce, such as Teriyaki, Honey BBQ and Hickory BBQ. Any favorite sauce, purchased or homemade, will work!

Oven Stew

2 pounds beef stew meat
1 cup chopped onion
2 cups sliced carrots
1 cup sliced mushrooms
1 (10.75-ounce) can beefy mushroom soup
1 (10.75-ounce) can golden mushroom soup

Cut beef stew meat into 1-inch cubes. Arrange stew meat, onion, carrots and mushrooms in a baking dish. Combine soups and pour over all. Cover tightly with extra heavy foil and bake for 3 hours at 325°. Remove from oven and allow to cool. Place in freezer bag. Label and freeze. 8 servings.

To serve: Thaw. Heat until hot and bubbly. Serve over hot mashed potatoes.

To prepare this recipe with potatoes, follow instructions above except bake for 2 hours at 325°. Cool, label, freeze.

To serve: Thaw. Add 3 diced potatoes. Cover and bake at 350° for 90 minutes.

Tomato Beef Stew

1 1/2 pounds beef stew meat
2 cups sliced carrots
1 cup sliced celery
3 tablespoons minced green bell pepper
1 cup chopped onion
2 (14.5-ounce) can diced tomatoes
1 (10.75-ounce) can tomato soup
1 teaspoon salt
1/8 teaspoon pepper

Cut beef stew meat into 1-inch cubes. Arrange stew meat, carrots, celery, green peppers and onion in a baking dish. Combine tomatoes, soup, salt and pepper and pour over all. Cover tightly with extra heavy foil and dish lid. Bake for 5 to 6 hours at 275°. Allow to cool. Place in freezer bag. Label and freeze. 6 servings.

To serve: Thaw. Heat until hot and bubbly. Serve with corn bread and honey butter.

To prepare this recipe with potatoes, follow instructions above except bake for 4 1/2 hours at 275°. Cool, label, freeze.

To serve: Thaw. Add 3 diced potatoes. Cover and bake at 350° for 90 minutes.

Porcupine Meatballs

1 pound lean ground beef
1/4 cup chopped onion
1/4 cup water
1/3 cup uncooked rice
1 (10.75-ounce) can tomato soup
1/2 teaspoon chili powder
1 teaspoon salt
1/2 cup water

Combine ground beef, onion, 1/4 cup water and uncooked rice. Shape into 1-inch balls. Arrange in greased baking dish. Combine soup, chili powder, salt and 1/2 cup water. Pour over meatballs. Cover and bake for 45 minutes at 350°. Remove from oven and allow to cool. Place in freezer bag. Label and freeze. 6 servings.

To Serve: Thaw. Heat until hot throughout.

This recipe may be frozen prior to baking. Prepare as above except place all in a freezer bag rather than in a baking dish. Label and freeze.

To serve: Thaw. Place in a greased baking dish. Bake covered at 350° for 1 hour.

Pineapple Meatballs

1 recipe **Basic Meatballs** (page 183)
3/4 cup barbeque sauce
3/4 cup orange juice
1/2 cup packed brown sugar
2 tablespoons cornstarch
1 (20-ounce) can crushed pineapple

Shape 1-inch balls from meatball recipe. Arrange meat-balls in greased baking dish. Combine barbeque sauce, orange juice, brown sugar, cornstarch and pineapple. Pour over meatballs. Bake covered for 45 minutes at 350°. Remove from oven and allow to cool. Place in freezer bag. Label and freeze. 6 servings.

To serve: Thaw. Heat until hot throughout. Serve with rice.

This recipe may be frozen prior to baking. Prepare as above except place all in a freezer bag rather than in a baking dish. Label and freeze.

To serve: Thaw. Place in a greased baking dish. Bake covered at 350° for 1 hour.

Meatballs in Gravy

1 recipe **Basic Meatballs** (page 183)
1 tablespoon flour
1 cup evaporated milk
1 (10.75-ounce) cream of chicken soup
1 tablespoon Worcestershire sauce
1 tablespoon sugar
1/2 teaspoon garlic salt
1/2 teaspoon onion salt

Shape 1-inch balls from meatball recipe. Arrange meat-balls in greased baking dish. Whisk flour into milk. Stir in soup, Worcestershire sauce, sugar, garlic salt and onion salt. Pour over meatballs. Bake covered for 45 minutes at 350°. Remove from oven and allow to cool. Place in freezer bag. Label and freeze. 6 servings.

To serve: Thaw. Heat until hot throughout. Serve over hot mashed potatoes or hot buttered noodles.

This recipe may be frozen prior to baking. Prepare as above except place all in a freezer bag rather than in a baking dish. Label and freeze.

To serve: Thaw. Place in a greased baking dish. Bake covered at 350° for 1 hour.

Calico Beans

1 pound ground beef
1 pound bacon, chopped
1 chopped onion
1 (15-ounce) can butter beans
1 (15-ounce) can red kidney beans
1 (15-ounce) can pork and beans
3/4 cup brown sugar
1/2 cup ketchup
2 teaspoons apple cider vinegar
1 teaspoon salt
1/2 teaspoon pepper

Brown ground beef and bacon with onion. Remove from heat. Add undrained butter beans, kidney beans and pork and beans. Stir in brown sugar, ketchup, vinegar, salt and pepper. Pour into greased baking dish. Bake uncovered at 350° for 1 hour. Remove from oven and allow to cool. Place in freezer bag. Label and freeze. 8 servings.

To serve: Thaw. Heat until hot throughout.

This recipe may be frozen prior to baking. Prepare as above except place all in a freezer bag rather than in a baking dish. Label and freeze.

To serve: Thaw. Place in a greased baking dish. Bake covered at 350° for 75 minutes.

Bacon Chicken

2 pounds boneless skinless chicken breast
6 slices bacon
1 (2.5-ounce) envelope pressed, sliced beef
1 (10.75-ounce) can cream of mushroom soup
2 cups sour cream

Snip the pressed beef into small strips and arrange on bottom of a greased foil baking pan. Cut chicken into 2-inch pieces and place on top of beef. Snip bacon into bite-sized pieces and place on top of chicken. Combine soup and sour cream. Pour over all. Bake uncovered at 275° for 2 hours. Remove from oven and allow to cool. Cover pan with extra heavy foil. Label and freeze. 6 servings.

To serve: Thaw. Bake covered at 350° for 1 hour. Serve over hot mashed potatoes or hot buttered noodles.

Peachy Chicken

1 (10.75-ounce) can tomato soup
1/2 cup honey
1/2 cup apple cider vinegar
1/2 cup brown sugar
2 tablespoons canola oil
1 tablespoon Worcestershire sauce
1 tablespoon ground mustard
1 teaspoon salt
1/4 teaspoon pepper
1/2 teaspoon garlic powder
2 pounds boneless skinless chicken breast
1 (29-ounce) can peach slices

In a saucepan, combine tomato soup, honey, vinegar, brown sugar, oil and Worcestershire sauce. Mix well. Whisk in ground mustard, salt, pepper and garlic powder. Bring to a boil. Reduce heat and simmer 15 minutes. Arrange chicken and drained peaches in greased baking dish. Pour sauce over chicken. Bake for 30 minutes at 350°. Turn chicken and bake 30 minutes longer, basting frequently. Remove from oven and allow to cool. Place in freezer bag. Label and freeze. 6 servings.

To serve: Thaw. Heat until sauce is bubbly and chicken is heated through. Delicious over rice.

———————————

This recipe may be frozen prior to baking. Prepare as above except place all in a freezer bag rather than in a baking dish. Label and freeze.

To serve: Thaw. Bake at 350° for 60 minutes, turning chicken after 30 minutes. Baste often.

Baked Chicken in Gravy

2 pounds boneless skinless chicken breast
1/4 cup flour
1/4 cup melted butter
6 slices American cheese
1 1/2 cups sliced mushrooms
1/4 cup minced onion
2/3 cup evaporated milk
1 (10.75-ounce) can cream of mushroom soup
1/2 teaspoon salt
1/4 teaspoon pepper

Coat chicken with flour. Pour melted butter into a foil baking pan. Place chicken in butter. Bake uncovered at 425° for 30 minutes. Turn chicken and bake 20 minutes longer. Remove from oven. Pour off liquid. Top chicken with cheese, mushrooms and onion. Combine milk, soup, salt and pepper. Pour over all. Allow to cool. Cover with extra heavy foil. Label and freeze. 6 servings.

To serve: Thaw: Bake covered at 350° for 45 minutes. Serve with rice or noodles.

Candied Chicken

2 pounds boneless skinless chicken breast
1/2 teaspoon salt
1/8 teaspoon pepper
1 1/2 cups maple syrup
3/4 cup apple cider vinegar
3/4 cup ketchup

Cut chicken into strips. Sprinkle chicken with salt and pepper. Place in greased baking dish. Bake 20 minutes at 350°. Pour off liquid. Combine syrup, vinegar and ketchup. Pour over chicken. Stir to coat. Bake uncovered 45 minutes at 350°. Baste chicken with sauce every 15 minutes. Remove from oven and allow to cool. Place in freezer bag. Label and freeze. 6 servings.

To serve: Thaw. Heat through. Serve with rice. Also delicious with baked potatoes.

If sauce is too thin, boil just the sauce on the stove top for a few minutes until the sauce thickens to your liking.

This recipe may be frozen prior to baking. Bake chicken 20 minutes and pour off liquid. Place chicken and sauce in freezer bag. Label and freeze.

To serve: Thaw. Bake uncovered at 350° for 1 hour, basting every 15 minutes.

Cranberry Chicken

2 pounds boneless skinless chicken breast
1 (16-ounce) can whole berry cranberry sauce
1 cup creamy French dressing
1 (1.25-ounce) envelope onion soup mix

Cut chicken into strips. Place in greased baking dish. Bake 20 minutes at 350°. Pour off liquid. Combine cranberry sauce, dressing and onion soup mix. Pour over chicken. Bake uncovered for 30 minutes at 350°. Remove from oven and allow to cool. Place in freezer bag. Label and freeze. 6 servings.

To serve: Thaw. Heat until hot throughout. Serve with rice.

For variations of this recipe, substitute other favorite dressings, such as Catalina, French or Russian, for the creamy French dressing.

This recipe may be frozen prior to baking. Bake chicken 20 minutes and pour off liquid. Place chicken and sauce in freezer bag. Label and freeze.

To serve: Thaw. Bake uncovered at 350° for 45 minutes.

Hawaiian Chicken

2 pounds boneless skinless chicken breast
1 (1.25-ounce) envelope onion soup mix
1 cup pineapple apricot jam
1 cup Russian salad dressing

Cut chicken into strips. Arrange chicken in greased baking dish. Bake 20 minutes at 350°. Pour off liquid. Combine onion soup, jam and dressing. Pour over chicken. Bake uncovered for 30 minutes at 350°. Remove from oven and allow to cool. Place in freezer bag. Label and freeze. 6 servings.

To serve: Thaw. Heat until hot and bubbly. Serve with rice.

This recipe may be frozen prior to baking. Bake chicken 20 minutes and pour off liquid. Place chicken and sauce in freezer bag. Label and freeze.

To serve: Thaw. Bake uncovered at 350° for 45 minutes.

Teriyaki Chicken

2 pounds boneless skinless chicken breast
3/4 cup soy sauce
1 cup sugar
3 tablespoon red wine vinegar
2 teaspoons sesame oil
2 teaspoons minced garlic
1 1/2 teaspoons minced ginger
1/4 cup cornstarch

Cut chicken into bite-sized pieces. Arrange in a greased baking dish. Bake for 15 minutes at 350°. Pour off liquid. In a saucepan, combine soy sauce, sugar, vinegar, oil, garlic, ginger and cornstarch. Cook and stir until thick and glossy. Pour over chicken in baking dish. Bake uncovered for 20 minutes at 350°. Remove from oven and allow to cool. Place in freezer bag. Label and freeze. 6 servings.

To serve: Thaw. Heat until hot and bubbly. Serve with rice and egg rolls.

This recipe may be frozen prior to baking. Bake chicken 15 minutes and pour off liquid. Place chicken and sauce in freezer bag. Label and freeze.

To serve: Thaw. Bake uncovered at 350° for 30 minutes.

Smoky Maple Chicken

1 cup sliced onion
2 pounds boneless skinless chicken breast
2 teaspoons hickory smoked salt
3/4 cup maple syrup
3/4 cup ketchup
2 tablespoons mustard
1/4 cup white vinegar
1 teaspoon Worcestershire sauce
1/8 teaspoon pepper

Place onions on bottom of greased baking dish. Cut chicken into serving-sized pieces and place on top of onion. Sprinkle chicken with hickory smoked salt. Bake at 350° for 20 minutes. Pour off liquid. Combine maple syrup, ketchup, mustard, vinegar, Worcestershire sauce and pepper. Pour over chicken. Bake uncovered at 350° for 30 minutes. Remove from oven and allow to cool. Place in freezer bag. Label and freeze. 6 servings.

To serve: Thaw. Heat until hot throughout. Serve with rice.

This recipe may be frozen prior to baking. Bake chicken and onions for 20 minutes and pour off liquid. Pour sauce over chicken. Freeze in foil baking pan covered with extra heavy foil.

To serve: Thaw. Bake uncovered at 350° for 45 minutes.

Cornflake Chicken

6 boneless skinless chicken breast halves
1/2 cup evaporated milk
1 cup corn flake crumbs
1 teaspoon salt
dash pepper
3 tablespoons butter

Spray baking sheet with non-stick cooking spray. Place 6 pats of butter on baking sheet. Dip chicken pieces first in evaporated milk, then in corn flake crumbs. Place each on a butter pat. Sprinkle with salt and pepper and top each with another butter pat. Bake for 30 minutes at 350°. Remove from oven and allow to cool. Cover chicken on baking sheet with plastic wrap. Place in freezer. Allow to freeze at least 3 hours. When frozen remove from baking sheet and place in freezer bag. Label and freeze. 6 servings.

To serve: Thaw. Heat through in microwave or covered in oven. Do not over bake.

To quickly and easily make corn flake crumbs, place corn flakes in a food processor. Pulse a few times until flakes are crushed to the desired size.

Chicken Cordon Bleu

6 small boneless skinless chicken breast halves
2 tablespoons Dijon mustard
6 slices ham
6 slices Swiss cheese
1 teaspoon salt
1/4 teaspoon pepper
1/2 cup evaporated milk
1 cup dry bread crumbs

Place each chicken breast half between two pieces of plastic wrap. Pound until thin. Spread 1 teaspoon mustard on each piece of chicken. Wrap cheese in ham and place on chicken. Roll chicken around cheese and ham. Secure with a toothpick. Dip chicken first in evaporated milk then in bread crumbs. Sprinkle with salt and pepper. Bake on greased baking sheet for 10 minutes at 400°. Reduce heat to 350° and bake an additional 25 minutes. Remove from oven and allow to cool. Cover chicken on baking sheet with plastic wrap. Freeze for at least 3 hours. When frozen transfer to freezer bag. Label and freeze. 6 servings.

To serve: Thaw. Heat in microwave or in oven. Do not over bake.

 Serve with chicken gravy made from 1 can cream of chicken soup and 1/2 cup sour cream.

StoveTop Recipes

Beef and Pork Chop Suey, 129
Beefy Spanish Rice, 128
Cabbage Patch Stew, 130
Cantonese Meatballs, 123
Chicken à la King, 145
Chicken and Mushrooms, 147
Chicken Fried Steak, 151
Chicken Ham Roll-Ups, 148
Chicken Stroganoff, 146
Chicken Tortellini Soup, 135
Chili, 124
Chili Soup, 125
Cola Chicken, 150
Corn Chowder, 136
Hawaiian Meatballs, 142
Honey Lime Chicken, 143
Italian Chili, 134
Jack Soup, 126
Lasagna, 121
Maple Almond Beef, 140
Meatball Soup, 138
Meatball Spaghetti, 122
Mexican Beef Stew, 133
Pork Chops, Carrots and Gravy, 154
Ravioli Soup, 120
Salisbury Steak and Gravy, 139
Skillet Barbeque Chicken, 153
Skillet Barbeque Pork Chops, 149
Southwest Stew, 131
Spaghetti Sauce, 119
Sweet and Sour Chicken, 144
Sweet and Sour Meatballs, 141
Taco Soup, 132
Teriyaki Beef, 137
Tomato Stroganoff, 127
Waikiki Turkey, 152

Spaghetti Sauce

1/2 pound ground beef
1/2 pound hot Italian sausage
2 cups chopped onion
4 teaspoons minced garlic
1 (12-ounce) tomato paste
3 (28-ounce) cans Italian tomatoes
2 cups water
4 bay leaves
3 tablespoons sugar
2 tablespoons Italian seasoning
2 teaspoons salt

Brown ground beef and sausage with onion and garlic. Stir in tomato paste, Italian tomatoes, water, bay leaves, sugar, Italian seasoning and salt. Bring to a boil. Reduce heat and simmer for 2 hours, stirring occasionally. Allow to cool. Remove bay leaves. Place in freezer bag(s) for spaghetti and/or pizza. Label and freeze. Or use to make other Italian recipes such as lasagna, manicotti or ravioli. 12 servings.

To serve: Thaw. Heat until hot and bubbly. Serve over hot pasta. Also makes wonderful pizza.

Use this sauce in recipes that call for spaghetti sauce, such as **Cheese Manicotti** (page 162), **Chicken Stuffed Manicotti** (page 163) and **Simply Lasagna** (page 164).

Ravioli Soup

1/2 pound ground beef
1/2 pound ground pork
1 cup chopped onion
2 teaspoons minced garlic
1 (28-ounce) can Italian tomatoes
1 (12-ounce) can tomato paste
2 (14.5-ounce) cans beef broth
1 tablespoon sugar
1 teaspoon Italian seasoning
1/4 cup dry bread crumbs
1/2 cup shredded fresh Parmesan cheese
1 (12-ounce) package frozen ravioli

Brown beef and pork with onion and garlic. Combine tomatoes, tomato paste, beef broth, sugar, Italian seasoning and dry bread crumbs. Bring to a boil. Reduce heat and simmer 30 minutes. Stir in Parmesan cheese. Allow to cool. Place in freezer bag or container. Freeze ravioli separately. Label and freeze. 8 servings.

To serve: Thaw. Cook ravioli according to package directions. Heat soup just to a boil. Add cooked ravioli. Serve with garlic bread and Parmesan cheese.

Ravioli Soup is especially delicious made with sausage filled ravioli. Try all the available types of frozen ravioli and see which you prefer.

Lasagna

1/2 pound lean ground beef
1/2 pound Italian sausage
1 cup chopped onion
1 (14.5-ounce) can Italian tomatoes
1 teaspoon minced garlic
1 (10.75-ounce) tomato soup
1 tablespoon dried parsley flakes
1 tablespoon sugar
1 teaspoon salt
2 tablespoon basil
1 cup Ricotta cheese
1 cup cottage cheese
1/4 cup shredded fresh Parmesan cheese
1 teaspoon dried parsley flakes
1/2 teaspoon oregano
4 cups shredded Mozzarella cheese
1/2 cup shredded fresh Parmesan cheese
12 lasagna noodles uncooked

Brown ground beef and sausage with onion. Add tomatoes, garlic, soup, 1 tablespoon parsley, sugar, salt and basil. Heat to boiling. Reduce heat, simmer for 1 hour. Mix Ricotta, cottage cheese, 1/4 cup Parmesan, 1 teaspoon parsley and oregano. Reserve 1/2 cup meat sauce for top. In ungreased foil baking pan, make 3 layers each of sauce, uncooked noodles, cheese mixture and mozzarella cheese. Spread reserved sauce over top. Sprinkle with Parmesan cheese. Cover with extra heavy foil. Label and freeze. 12 servings.

To serve: Thaw. Bake uncovered for 1 hour at 350°.

Meatball Spaghetti

1 recipe **Basic Meatballs** (page 183)
1 pound Italian sausage links
1 cup chopped onion
1 cup chopped green bell pepper
2 (14.5-ounce) cans Italian tomatoes
2 (8-ounce) cans tomato sauce
1 (14.5-ounce) can beef broth
1 (6-ounce) can tomato paste
2 teaspoons minced garlic
2 teaspoons basil
2 teaspoons oregano
2 teaspoons dried parsley flakes
2 tablespoons sugar
1 teaspoon salt
1/4 teaspoon pepper

Shape 3/4-inch balls from meatball recipe. Brown on all sides or bake at 350° for 5 minutes. (Meatballs do not need to be cooked through.) Cut sausage in pieces and brown with onion and bell pepper. Add tomatoes, tomato sauce, beef broth, tomato paste, garlic, basil, oregano, parsley, sugar, salt and pepper. Gently stir in meatballs. Bring to a boil. Reduce heat. Cover and simmer for 2 1/2 hours. Allow to cool. Place in freezer bag. Label and freeze. 10 servings.

To serve: Thaw. Heat until hot and bubbly. Serve over hot spaghetti.

Cantonese Meatballs

1 recipe **Basic Meatballs** (page 183)
1 (20-ounce) can pineapple chunks
1/2 cup packed brown sugar
1/2 cup teriyaki sauce
2 tablespoons red wine vinegar
1/4 cup ketchup
1/4 cup cornstarch

Shape 1-inch balls from meatball recipe. Brown on all sides or bake at 350° for 7 minutes. (Meatballs do not need to be cooked through.) Drain pineapple reserving juice. Combine reserved pineapple juice, brown sugar, teriyaki sauce, vinegar, ketchup and cornstarch. Cook and stir until thick and bubbly. Add meatballs and simmer 10 minutes. Remove from heat and add pineapple. Allow to cool. Place in freezer bag. Label and freeze. 6 servings.

To serve: Thaw. Pour into skillet and heat until bubbly. Serve with rice.

Chili

2 pounds ground beef
1 cup chopped onion
1 cup chopped green bell pepper
1 cup chopped celery
1 teaspoon minced garlic
1 tablespoon Worcestershire sauce
1 tablespoon chili powder
1 (15-ounce) can pinto beans
1 (15-ounce) can small red beans
1 (15-ounce) can pork and beans
2 tablespoons sugar
2 (14.5-ounce) cans diced tomatoes
1 (15-ounce) can tomato sauce
1 teaspoon salt
1/2 teaspoon pepper

Brown ground beef with onion. Add bell pepper, celery, garlic, Worcestershire sauce and chili powder. Stir in undrained beans, sugar, tomatoes, tomato sauce, salt and pepper. Heat to a boil. Reduce heat and simmer for 2 hours. Allow to cool. Place in freezer bag or container. Label and freeze. 8 servings.

To serve: Thaw. Heat until hot and bubbly. Serve with corn bread and honey butter.

Chili Soup

1 pound ground beef
1 cup chopped onion
2 (14.5-ounce) cans diced tomatoes
1 (15-ounce) can small red beans
1 teaspoon minced garlic
1 cup sliced celery
1 cup sliced carrots
1 1/2 teaspoons chili powder
2 teaspoons salt
1 tablespoon sugar
1/2 teaspoon pepper
1 cup sliced zucchini

Brown ground beef with onion. Add tomatoes, undrained beans, garlic, celery and carrots. Stir in chili powder, salt, sugar and pepper. Bring to a boil. Reduce heat and simmer for 2 hours. Add zucchini and simmer 10 minutes more. Allow to cool. Place in freezer bag or container. Label and freeze. 6 servings.

To serve: Thaw. Heat soup to boiling. Serve with shredded fresh Parmesan cheese and crusty bread.

Jack Soup

1 pound ground beef
2 cups chopped onion
4 cups water
2 (14.5-ounce) cans diced tomatoes
2 cups sliced carrots
1 teaspoon salt
1 bay leaf
2 cups cubed Monterey Jack cheese

Brown ground beef with onion. Add water, tomatoes, carrots, salt and bay leaf. Heat to boiling. Reduce heat and simmer 1 1/2 hours. Allow to cool. Remove bay leaf. (Do not add cheese until serving.) Place in freezer bag or container. Label and freeze. 6 servings.

To serve: Thaw. Heat just to boiling. Remove from heat and add cheese. Serve with cheese partially melted.

 Cheese may be cubed and placed in a small freezer bag and frozen with soup.

Tomato Stroganoff

1 pound ground beef
1/2 cup chopped onion
2 tablespoons flour
1 tablespoon sugar
1/2 teaspoon basil
1/2 teaspoon salt
1/8 teaspoon garlic powder
1/8 teaspoon pepper
1 (10.5-ounce) can beef broth
1 (6-ounce) tomato paste
1 1/2 cups sliced mushrooms
1 cup sour cream

Brown ground beef with onion. Remove from heat. Add flour, sugar, basil, salt, garlic powder and pepper. Mix well. Stir in beef broth, tomato paste and mushrooms. Return to heat and simmer 10 minutes, stirring occasionally until thickened. Remove from heat. Allow to cool. Stir in sour cream. Place in freezer bag. Label and freeze. 6 servings.

To serve: Thaw. Heat just until hot throughout. Serve over hot buttered noodles.

Beefy Spanish Rice

1 pound ground beef
1 cup chopped onion
1/2 cup chopped green bell pepper
1 teaspoon minced garlic
2 tablespoons butter
1 cup uncooked rice
2 1/2 cups beef broth
1 teaspoon salt
2 teaspoons sugar
1 teaspoon chili powder
1/4 teaspoon pepper

Brown ground beef with onion, bell pepper and garlic. Remove from skillet. Melt butter in skillet and stir in rice. Cook and stir rice for about 5 minutes, until golden. Return beef and vegetables to pan. Add beef broth, salt, sugar, chili powder and pepper. Cover and simmer about 30 minutes, stirring occasionally. Allow to cool. Place in freezer bag. Label and freeze. 6 servings.

To serve: Thaw. Heat through.

Beef and Pork Chop Suey

1/2 pound lean beef, cubed
1/4 pound lean pork, cubed
2 tablespoons olive oil
1 cup chopped onion
1 teaspoon minced garlic
3 cups beef broth
1 teaspoon salt
2 tablespoons brown sugar
2 tablespoons Worcestershire sauce
2 tablespoons soy sauce
1/2 cup sliced carrot
1 (8-ounce) can sliced water chestnuts
1 cup sliced celery
1 cup bean sprouts
3 tablespoons cornstarch
1/2 cup cold water

Brown beef and pork in olive oil with onion and garlic. Stir in beef broth, salt, brown sugar, Worcestershire sauce, soy sauce, carrot, drained water chestnuts, celery and sprouts. Cover and simmer slowly for 45 minutes, stirring occasionally. Dissolve cornstarch in cold water. Stir into simmering chop suey. Cook and stir until thickened. Allow to cool. Place in freezer bag. Label and freeze. 6 servings.

To serve: Thaw. Heat until bubbly. Serve over rice and chow mein noodles.

Cabbage Patch Stew

2 pounds ground beef
1 cup chopped onion
1 1/2 cups sliced celery
2 (15-ounce) cans kidney beans
3 cups shredded cabbage
2 cups beef broth
2 (14.5-ounce) cans diced tomatoes
1 tablespoon chili powder
2 tablespoons sugar
2 teaspoon salt
1 tablespoon Worcestershire sauce

Brown ground beef with onion and celery. Add undrained beans. Stir in cabbage, beef broth, tomatoes, chili powder, sugar, salt and Worcestershire sauce. Bring to a boil. Reduce heat, cover and simmer 1 hour. Allow to cool. Place in freezer bag or container. Label and freeze. 8 servings.

To serve: Thaw. Bring soup to a boil. Serve with bread and butter.

Southwest Stew

1 pound ground beef
1 cup chopped onion
1 teaspoon minced garlic
2 (14.5-ounce) cans Mexican tomatoes
1 cup frozen corn
1 (15-ounce) can pinto beans
1 cup picante sauce
3/4 cup beef broth
1 teaspoon cumin
1/4 teaspoon pepper
1 teaspoon salt

Brown ground beef with onion and garlic. Add tomatoes, corn, undrained beans, picante sauce, beef broth, cumin, pepper and salt. Bring to a boil. Reduce heat, cover and simmer 30 minutes. Remove from heat. Allow to cool. Place in freezer bag. Label and freeze. 6 servings.

To serve: Thaw. Heat to boiling. Top each serving with shredded Cheddar cheese.

 Any thick, chunky salsa may be substituted for the picante sauce.

Taco Soup

1 pound ground beef
1 cup chopped onion
1/2 cup chopped green bell pepper
1 teaspoon minced garlic
2 (15-ounce) cans pinto beans
2 (14.5-ounce) cans diced tomatoes
1 cup water
1 (4-ounce) can diced green chiles
1 (8-ounce) can tomato sauce
1 (1.25-ounce) envelope taco seasoning

Brown ground beef with onion. Add bell pepper, garlic, undrained beans, tomatoes, water, green chiles, tomato sauce and taco seasoning. Heat to boiling. Reduce heat and simmer 1 hour. Allow to cool. Place in freezer bag or container. Label and freeze. 6 servings.

To serve: Thaw. Heat until hot and bubbly. Serve with tortilla chips.

Mexican Beef Stew

2 pounds beef stew meat
2 tablespoons canola oil
1 cup chopped onion
1 teaspoon minced garlic
1 (4-ounce) can diced green chiles
1 (14.5-ounce) can Mexican tomatoes
1/2 teaspoon cumin
1 tablespoon sugar
1 teaspoon salt
1/4 teaspoon pepper

Cut beef stew meat into 1-inch cubes. Brown beef over medium-high heat in oil with onion and garlic. Stir in green chiles, tomatoes, cumin, sugar, salt and pepper. Heat to boiling. Reduce heat. Cover and simmer 2 hours. Add water during cooking, if necessary. Allow to cool. Place in freezer bag. Label and freeze. 8 servings.

To serve: Thaw. Heat to boiling. Serve with cheese quesadillas.

Italian Chili

1 pound ground beef
1 cup chopped onion
1 teaspoon minced garlic
1 cup sliced mushrooms
1 (26-ounce) jar spaghetti sauce
1 1/2 cups beef broth
1 (14.5-ounce) can Italian tomatoes
1 (2-ounce) package sliced pepperoni
1 tablespoon chili powder
1 tablespoon sugar

Brown ground beef with onion, garlic and mushrooms. Stir in spaghetti sauce, beef broth, tomatoes, pepperoni, chili powder and sugar. Bring to a boil. Reduce heat and simmer, uncovered, for 30 minutes. Allow to cool. Place in freezer bag. Label and freeze. 6 servings.

To serve: Thaw. Heat to boiling. Serve with crusty bread or garlic toast.

Chicken Tortellini Soup

2 quarts chicken broth
1 1/2 pounds boneless skinless chicken breast
1 cup chopped onion
1 tablespoon dried parsley flakes
1 1/2 sliced carrots
1/2 cup sliced celery
1 teaspoon salt
2 cups frozen tortellini

Combine chicken broth, chicken, onion, dried parsley flakes, carrots, celery and salt. Bring to a boil. Reduce heat and simmer for 1 1/2 hours. Remove from heat and allow to cool. Remove chicken and shred or chop. Return to soup. Place in freezer bag or container. Freeze tortellini separately. Label and freeze. 6 servings.

To serve: Thaw. Heat to boiling. Add tortellini and continue to boil for the time recommended on tortellini package. Serve with hot rolls and butter.

 Frozen tortellini come in several different fillings. Try this soup with cheese filled tortellini.

Corn Chowder

1/2 pound bacon, chopped
1 1/2 cups chopped onion
1 cup sliced celery
1 bay leaf
1/4 cup flour
5 cups water
4 cups diced potatoes
2 (15-ounce) cans creamed corn
2 cups half-and-half
4 cups chicken broth
2 tablespoons butter
1 teaspoon salt
1/2 teaspoon pepper

Cook bacon until crisp. Drain on paper towels. Drain all but 1/4 cup drippings. Add onions and celery to drippings and cook until soft. Add bay leaf. Stir in flour. Cook 3 minutes. Add 5 cups water and potatoes. Bring to a boil. Simmer 30 minutes. Stir in corn, half-and-half, chicken broth, butter, salt and pepper. Heat just until butter melts. Allow to cool. Remove bay leaf. Place in freezer bag or container. Label and freeze. 8 servings.

To serve: Heat and stir just until smooth and hot throughout. Thin with broth or milk, if necessary.

Teriyaki Beef

2 pounds beef sirloin steak
3 tablespoons sesame oil
2 cups water
2/3 cup soy sauce
2 tablespoons sugar
1/2 teaspoon pepper
2 teaspoon minced garlic
3 tablespoons cornstarch
1/2 cup water
1 cup thin carrot strips
1 1/2 cups sliced mushrooms
1 1/2 cups sliced green bell peppers
1 cup sliced onion
1 (8-ounce) can sliced water chestnuts

Cut steak, across grain, into thin strips and brown in oil. Add water, soy sauce, sugar, pepper and garlic. Cover and simmer 45 minutes. Dissolve cornstarch in 1/2 cup water. Stir into sauce. Cook and stir until thick. Add carrot strips and mushrooms. Simmer gently 2 minutes. Remove from heat. Add bell peppers, onions and drained water chestnuts. Allow to cool. Place in freezer bag. Label and freeze. 8 servings.

To serve: Thaw. Heat until hot and bubbly. Serve with hot rice.

Meatball Soup

1 recipe **Basic Meatballs** (page 183)
4 cups water
1 (1.25-ounce) envelope onion soup mix
1 (14.5-ounce) can diced tomatoes
1 (15-ounce) can kidney beans
1 cup diced carrots
1 cup uncooked rice
1 tablespoon sugar
1/4 teaspoon pepper

Shape 1/2-inch balls from Basic Meatball recipe. Brown on all sides or bake at 350° for 4 minutes. (Meatballs do not need to be cooked through.) In a large saucepan, combine water, onion soup mix, tomatoes, undrained beans, carrots, rice, sugar and pepper. Bring to a boil. Add meatballs. Reduce heat and simmer 25 minutes. Remove from heat. Allow to cool. Place in freezer bag. Label and freeze. 8 servings.

To serve: Thaw. Heat to boiling. Serve with garlic toast.

Salisbury Steak and Gravy

1 (10.75-ounce) can French Onion soup
1 1/2 pounds lean ground beef
1/2 cup dry bread crumbs
1 egg, slightly beaten
1/2 teaspoon salt
1/8 teaspoon pepper
1 tablespoon flour
1/4 cup ketchup
1/4 cup water
1 teaspoon Worcestershire sauce
1/2 teaspoon mustard

Combine 1/3 cup soup, ground beef, crumbs, egg, salt and pepper. Shape into 6 oval patties. Brown on both sides and remove from pan. Combine remaining soup, flour, ketchup, water, Worcestershire sauce and mustard in skillet. Stir together and loosen bits on bottom of pan. Return patties to pan and cover. Cook over low heat for 20 minutes, stirring occasionally. Remove from heat and allow to cool. Place in freezer bag. Label and freeze. 6 servings.

To serve: Thaw. Heat until steaks are hot throughout and gravy is bubbly. Serve over hot mashed potatoes.

Maple Almond Beef

2 pounds beef sirloin steak
2 tablespoons olive oil
1/2 cup sliced onion
1/2 cup sliced green bell pepper
1/2 cup sliced red bell pepper
2 teaspoons minced garlic
1/3 cup red wine vinegar
1/2 cup maple syrup
2 tablespoons soy sauce
2 tablespoons cornstarch
1/2 cup slivered almonds

Cut partially frozen steak into thin strips. Brown steak in oil with onion, peppers and garlic. In a separate bowl, combine vinegar, syrup, soy sauce and cornstarch. Stir into beef. Cook and stir until thickened. Allow to cool. (Do not add almonds until serving.) Place in freezer bag. Label and freeze. 8 servings.

To serve: Thaw. Heat through. Top with slivered almonds. Serve with hot white rice.

 Almonds may be frozen in a separate bag, along with the Maple Almond Beef.

Sweet and Sour Meatballs

1 recipe **Basic Meatballs** (page 183)
1/2 cup packed brown sugar
2 tablespoons cornstarch
1 cup water
1/4 teaspoon salt
1/2 cup apple cider vinegar
1/4 cup ketchup
1/2 cup chunked onion
1/2 cup chunked red bell pepper
1/2 cup chunked green bell pepper

Shape 1-inch balls from meatball recipe. Brown on all sides or bake at 350° for 7 minutes. (Meatballs do not need to be cooked through.) Mix together brown sugar and cornstarch. Add water, salt, vinegar and ketchup. Heat to boiling. Reduce heat. Cook and stir until thick and bubbly. Add meatballs and simmer 15 minutes. Stir in onion, red pepper and green pepper. Remove from heat and allow to cool. Place in freezer bag. Label and freeze. 6 servings.

To serve: Thaw. Heat to boiling and simmer 10 minutes. Serve with hot rice.

If you prefer your onions and peppers stir-fry crunchy, do not add them before freezing. Stir-fry the vegetables and add them to the sauce at serving time.

Hawaiian Meatballs

1 recipe **Basic Meatballs** (page 183)
1 cup brown sugar
1/4 cup cornstarch
2 cups pineapple juice
1/2 teaspoon minced ginger
1 teaspoon salt
1/2 cup apple cider vinegar
2 tablespoons soy sauce
1 cup chunked green bell pepper
1 (20-ounce) can pineapple chunks

Shape 1-inch balls from meatball recipe. Brown on all sides or bake at 350° for 7 minutes. (Meatballs do not need to be cooked through.) Combine brown sugar and cornstarch. Stir in pineapple juice, ginger, salt, vinegar and soy sauce. Cook and stir until thick and clear. Add bell pepper, pineapple and meatballs. Simmer 15 minutes. Allow to cool. Place in freezer bag. Label and freeze. 6 servings.

To serve: Thaw. Heat until sauce is hot and bubbly and meatballs are heated through. Serve over hot rice.

If you prefer your onions and peppers stir-fry crunchy, do not add them before freezing. Stir-fry the vegetables and add them at serving time.

Honey Lime Chicken

2 pounds chicken tenders
1 1/2 teaspoons garlic salt
1 tablespoon peanut oil
1 (20-ounce) can pineapple rings
1/4 cup honey
3 tablespoons lime juice
2 tablespoons soy sauce
1 tablespoon cornstarch

Sprinkle chicken with garlic salt. Brown in oil. Drain pineapple, reserving juice. Add 1/4 cup of reserved pineapple juice to skillet. Cover and simmer 6 to 8 minutes, until chicken is golden. Remove chicken. Add honey, lime juice, soy sauce, cornstarch and remainder of pineapple juice. Bring to boil. Cook and stir until thick and clear, about 1 minute. Remove from heat. Allow to cool. Place chicken, pineapple rings and sauce in freezer bag. Label and freeze. 6 servings.

To serve: Thaw. Heat until sauce is hot and bubbly and chicken is heated through. Serve over hot rice and garnish with lime wedges.

To easily juice a lime, heat lime in the microwave in a glass bowl until the lime bursts (about 1 minute). Immediately stop microwave and allow lime to cool briefly. Lime juice can then be squeezed easily from the hole made by the escaping steam.

Sweet and Sour Chicken

2 pounds boneless skinless chicken breast
1 tablespoon canola oil
1/2 cup sliced carrot
1 teaspoon minced garlic
1 cup sugar
1/4 cup cornstarch
1 1/3 cups water
3 tablespoons canola oil
2/3 cup apple cider vinegar
4 tablespoons soy sauce
1 cup chunked onion
1/2 cup chunked red bell pepper
1/2 cup chunked green bell pepper
1 (8-ounce) can pineapple chunks, drained

Cut chicken in 1-inch cubes. Cook in oil with carrot and garlic until no longer pink. Remove from heat and allow to cool. Combine sugar and cornstarch in saucepan. Stir in water. Add oil, vinegar and soy sauce. Cook and stir until thick and clear. Remove from heat. Stir together chicken, sauce, vegetables and pineapple. Allow to cool. Place in freezer bag. Label and freeze. 6 servings.

To serve: Thaw. Heat until hot and bubbly. Serve with hot rice.

If you prefer your onions and peppers stir-fry crunchy, do not add them before freezing. Stir-fry the vegetables and add at serving time.

Chicken à la King

2 slices bacon, diced
1/4 cup chopped onion
1/2 cup chopped mushrooms
1 tablespoon minced green bell pepper
2 tablespoons butter
1/2 cup flour
1 teaspoon salt
1/4 teaspoon pepper
2 cups cream
1 1/3 cups chicken broth
2 cups cooked, chopped chicken

Cook bacon, onion, mushrooms and green pepper in butter until vegetables are soft and bacon is beginning to brown. Blend in flour, salt and pepper. Stir in cream and broth. Cook until bubbly. Continue to cook and stir 1 minute. Remove from heat and add chicken. Allow to cool. Place in freezer bag. Label and freeze. 6 servings.

To serve: Thaw. Heat in saucepan. Cook and stir until hot and bubbly. Serve over toast, biscuits or puff pastry.

Chicken Stroganoff

1 1/2 pounds boneless skinless chicken breast
2 tablespoons canola oil
2 tablespoons butter
2 cups sliced mushrooms
1 cup sliced onions
2 tablespoons flour
1 1/2 cups chicken broth
1 (10.75-ounce) can cream of mushroom soup
1 tablespoon sugar
1 cup sour cream
1 teaspoon red wine vinegar
1 teaspoon Dijon mustard
1/2 teaspoon salt
1/4 teaspoon pepper

Cut chicken in bite-sized pieces. Brown in oil. Remove from pan. Add butter to same pan. Cook mushrooms and onion in butter until liquid is gone. Whisk together flour and broth. Add to skillet. Cook and stir until thick and bubbly. Remove from heat. Add soup, sugar, sour cream, vinegar, mustard, salt, pepper and chicken. Allow to cool. Place in freezer bag. Label and freeze. 6 servings.

To serve: Thaw. Heat and stir until hot throughout. Serve over hot buttered noodles.

Chicken and Mushrooms

2 pounds boneless skinless chicken breast
1/4 cup cornstarch
2 tablespoons olive oil
1 1/2 cups sliced mushrooms
1 cup sliced onion
1/2 cup chicken broth
1/4 cup cream

Cut chicken in strips and coat with cornstarch. Brown in olive oil. Add mushrooms and onions and cook until limp. Stir in broth and cream. Cook and stir until slightly thickened. Remove from heat and allow to cool. Place in freezer bag. Label and freeze. 6 servings.

To serve: Thaw. Heat and sir until sauce is smooth, hot and bubbly and chicken is hot throughout. Serve over rice.

Chicken Ham Roll-Ups

6 small boneless skinless chicken breast halves
6 slices ham
3 tablespoons butter
1 (10.75-ounce) can cream of chicken soup
1/2 cup sour cream
1 teaspoon Worcestershire sauce

Place each chicken breast half between 2 pieces of plastic wrap. Pound until thin. Top each piece of chicken with a slice of ham. Roll up and secure with toothpicks. Heat butter in skillet. Lightly brown chicken on all sides. Allow to cool. Remove toothpicks. Arrange in a greased foil baking pan. Combine soup, sour cream and Worcestershire sauce. Pour sauce over chicken rolls. Label and freeze. 6 servings.

To serve: Thaw. Bake uncovered for 30 minutes at 350°.

Skillet Barbeque Pork Chops

6 pork chops
1 tablespoon canola oil
3/4 cup water
1/2 cup teriyaki sauce
1/2 cup ketchup
3 tablespoons brown sugar
2 tablespoons cornstarch
1/4 cup cold water

Brown chops in oil slowly on both sides. Combine 3/4 cup water, teriyaki sauce, ketchup and brown sugar. Pour over chops. Cover and simmer 30 minutes. Turn over and simmer 20 minutes more. Remove chops from pan. Dissolve cornstarch in cold water. Stir into simmering sauce. Cook and stir until thickened and bubbly. Allow to cool. Place chops and sauce in freezer bag. Label and freeze. 6 servings.

To serve: Thaw. Heat until chops are hot throughout and sauce is bubbly.

Cola Chicken

2 pounds boneless skinless chicken breast
1 cup chopped onion
2 tablespoons canola oil
1 (12-ounce) can cola flavored soda
1 cup ketchup
1 teaspoon minced garlic
1 teaspoon salt
1/2 teaspoon pepper
2 tablespoons cornstarch
1/4 cup cold water

Cut chicken into strips. Brown chicken and onion in oil. Add cola, ketchup, garlic, salt and pepper. Cover and simmer 30 minutes. Remove chicken. Dissolve cornstarch in cold water. Stir into simmering sauce. Cook and stir until thickened and bubbly. Allow to cool. Place chicken and sauce in freezer bag. Label and freeze. 6 servings.

To serve: Thaw. Heat until chicken is hot throughout and sauce is bubbly.

Chicken Fried Steak

1/2 cup flour
1/2 teaspoon salt
1/4 teaspoon pepper
1 1/2 pounds beef cube steaks
1/2 cup buttermilk
1 cup crushed butter crackers
1/4 cup canola oil
1 (10.75-ounce) can beefy mushroom soup
1/2 cup evaporated milk
1/2 cup milk
2 teaspoon sugar

Combine flour, salt and pepper. Cut meat into serving-sized pieces. Coat steaks with flour mixture, then dip in buttermilk, then coat with cracker crumbs. Brown steaks quickly in hot oil on both sides. Continue to cook over medium heat just until cooked through. Remove from heat and remove steaks. Stir in soup, evaporated milk, milk and sugar. Mix well and loosen bits from bottom of pan. Place cooled steaks and gravy in freezer bag. Label and freeze. 6 servings.

To serve: Thaw. Heat until steaks are hot throughout and gravy is bubbly. Serve with hot mashed potatoes.

For quick cracker crumbs, place coarsely broken crackers in a food processor. Pulse processor a few times until crumbs are the desired size.

Waikiki Turkey

3 cups diced turkey breast
1/2 cup chopped onion
1/2 cup chopped green bell pepper
3 tablespoons teriyaki sauce
1/2 cup thin carrot strips
1 cup pineapple juice
2 tablespoons apple cider vinegar
3 tablespoons soy sauce
1/2 cup brown sugar
2 tablespoons cornstarch
1/2 cup frozen pea pods
1/2 cup pineapple chunks

Cook turkey with onion and bell pepper in teriyaki sauce. Add carrots and cook 1 minute longer. Remove from skillet. Into same skillet, stir pineapple juice, vinegar, soy sauce, brown sugar and cornstarch. Cook and stir until thick and clear. Remove from heat and return turkey to skillet. Add pea pods, carrot, pineapple and turkey. Allow to cool. Place in freezer bag. Label and freeze. 6 servings.

To serve: Thaw. Heat until hot and bubbly. Serve over hot rice.

 Use a vegetable peeler to cut a carrot into thin, wide strips.

 For **Waikiki Chicken**, substitute 3 cups diced chicken breast for the turkey breast.

Skillet Barbeque Chicken

2 pounds boneless skinless chicken breast
1/3 cup brown sugar
1/3 cup white vinegar
1 cup ketchup
1/2 cup corn syrup
1 tablespoon Worcestershire sauce
1/2 teaspoon garlic salt
1/4 cup water
1/2 teaspoon celery seed
1 teaspoon salt
1 dash pepper

Cut chicken into serving-sized pieces. In a skillet or an electric skillet, combine brown sugar, vinegar, ketchup, corn syrup, Worcestershire sauce, garlic salt, water, celery seed, salt and pepper. Add chicken and turn to coat. Cover and simmer 35 minutes, turning chicken occasionally. Uncover and cook until sauce is thick and glossy. Allow to cool. Place in freezer bag. Label and freeze. 6 servings.

To serve: Thaw. Heat until chicken is hot throughout and sauce is hot and bubbly. Serve with rice, noodles or baked potatoes.

Pork Chops, Carrots and Gravy

6 pork chops
1/4 cup flour
1 cup chopped onion
1 tablespoons canola oil
2 (10.75-ounce) cans cream of chicken soup
1/2 teaspoon garlic salt
1 tablespoons Worcestershire sauce
2 1/2 cups water
1 tablespoon sugar
2 cups baby carrots

Coat chops with flour. Brown chops in oil with onion. Remove chops. Add soup, garlic salt, Worcestershire sauce, water and sugar. Whisk together until smooth. Return chops to pan and add carrots. Heat to boiling. Reduce heat, cover and simmer 1 hour. Allow to cool. Place in freezer bag. Label and freeze. 6 servings.

To serve: Thaw. Heat until hot throughout. Serve over boiled or mashed potatoes.

Assemble Recipes

Almost Ravioli, 160
Bacon Meat Loaf, 176
Barbeque Beef and Biscuits, 170
Basic Meatballs, 183
Beef and Broccoli, 192
Beef and Cheese Roll-Ups, 189
Beef Noodle Onion Bake, 168
Beef Stuffing Bake, 159
Beefy Chinese Rice, 188
Beefy Macaroni, 167
Bird's Nest Pie, 157
Biscuit Beef Bake, 169
Broccoli Chicken and Rice, 199
California Dip Meat Loaf, 180
Cheese Manicotti, 162
Cheesy Chicken and Rice, 202
Cheesy Ham and Noodles, 220
Cheesy Ham and Potatoes, 217
Cheesy Lasagna, 186
Cheesy Meat Loaf, 174
Chicken and Biscuits, 203
Chicken and Broccoli, 198
Chicken and Dressing, 201
Chicken and Ham Dinner, 211
Chicken and Rice, 204
Chicken Enchiladas, 209
Chicken Stuffed Manicotti, 163
Chili Beef and Rice, 190
Corkscrew Chicken, 196
Corny Meat Loaf, 179
Country Chicken and Vegetables, 207
Cowboy Barbeque, 171
Creamed Corn and Beef, 166
Creamy Chicken and Pasta, 212
Glazed Meat Loaf, 177
Green Chile Chicken Soup, 200
Ground Beef Stroganoff, 194
Ham and Chicken Roll-Ups, 210

continued...

Ham and Noodles, 216
Ham and Potato Scallop, 218
Ham Loaf with Pineapple Sauce, 214
Ham Primavera, 221
Italian Shells, 165
Mayonnaise Chicken, 206
Meatballs in Sour Cream Sauce, 184
Meat Loaf and Potatoes, 172
Mexican Lasagna, 187
Mock Filet Mignon, 195
Nacho Meat Loaf, 178
Navajo Tacos, 197
Onion Soup Meat Loaf, 175
Pizza in a Dish, 193
Pizza Meat Loaf, 173
Pork Chops and Potatoes, 222
Pork Loaf with Applesauce Glaze, 215
Scalloped Pork Chops, 223
Simply Lasagna, 164
Spaghetti and Company, 161
Spaghetti and Meatballs, 185
Steak and Vegetable Pie, 191
Stuffing Meat Loaves, 182
Swiss Ham and Noodles, 219
Taco Pie, 158
Tortilla Chicken, 208
Tuna Bow Ties, 224
Tuna Broccoli AuGratin, 228
Tuna Chow Mein, 227
Tuna Fettucinni, 225
Tuna Stroganoff, 226
Turkey and Stuffing Roll-Ups, 213
Turkey Dressing Pie, 205
Very Best Meat Loaf, 181

Bird's Nest Pie

1 (8-ounce) package spaghetti noodles
2 eggs, beaten
1/3 cup canned Parmesan cheese
3 tablespoons melted butter
1 tablespoon dried parsley flakes
1 cup sour cream
1 (3-ounce) package softened cream cheese
1 cup shredded Mozzarella cheese
1 pound Italian sausage
1/2 cup chopped onion
1 (6-ounce) Italian tomato paste
1 cup water

Cook spaghetti noodles in boiling, salted water for the shortest time recommended on package. Drain. Mix warm spaghetti with eggs, Parmesan, butter and parsley. Press into a greased foil pie pan. Mix sour cream and cream cheese. Spread on top of spaghetti crust. Sprinkle with Mozzarella. Brown sausage with onion. Add tomato paste and water. Simmer 10 minutes. Pour on top of cheese. Cover with extra heavy foil. Label and freeze. 6 servings.

To serve: Thaw. Bake covered for 45 minutes at 350°. Uncover. Top with Mozzarella cheese. Bake 5 minutes.

 For interesting pasta crust variations, substitute other pasta shapes for the spaghetti noodles.

Taco Pie

1 pound lean ground beef
1 cup chopped onion
1 (1.25-ounce) envelope taco seasoning
1 (2.25-ounce) can sliced black olives
1 (8-ounce) can tomato sauce
1 (8-ounce) can refrigerated crescent roll dough
1 cup refried beans
2 cups shredded Cheddar cheese, divided
1 (10 1/2-ounce) bag corn chips, coarsely crushed
1 cup sour cream

Brown ground beef with onion. Add taco seasoning, drained olives and tomato sauce. Unroll crescent roll dough and press together perforations. Press onto bottom and up sides of a foil baking pan. Heat refried beans and mix with 2 tablespoons of water to make spreadable. Spread over crust. Top with 1 cup of cheese. Cover crust with half of the crushed corn chips. Spoon meat mixture over corn chips. Cover with sour cream. Sprinkle with remaining 1 cup of cheese. Top with remaining corn chips. Cover with extra heavy foil. Label and Freeze. 8 servings.

To serve: Thaw. Bake uncovered 45 minutes at 375°.

Beef Stuffing Bake

1 pound lean ground beef
1 cup chopped onion
1 (10.75-ounce) can cream of celery soup
1 (10.75-ounce) can cream of mushroom soup
1 (10-ounce) box beef stuffing mix
1 cup water
1 cup sliced mushrooms
1 cup frozen peas and carrots

Brown beef with onion. Place in a greased foil baking pan. Whisk together soups and water. Add seasoning mix from stuffing mix. Stir in mushrooms, peas and carrots. Sprinkle stuffing mix over beef. Pour soup mixture over all. Cover with extra heavy foil. Label and freeze. 8 servings.

To serve: Thaw. Bake uncovered for 45 minutes at 350°.

Almost Ravioli

1 pound lean ground beef
1 cup chopped onion
1 teaspoon minced garlic
3 cups uncooked bow tie pasta
1 (26-ounce) jar spaghetti sauce
1 (8-ounce) can tomato sauce
1/4 teaspoon pepper
2 tablespoons sugar
1 (10-ounce) package frozen chopped spinach
1 cup cottage cheese
2 eggs, slightly beaten
1/2 cup shredded fresh Parmesan cheese

Brown ground beef with onion and garlic. Cook bow tie pasta in boiling, salted water for 2 minutes less than the shortest time recommended on package. Drain. Add pasta to ground beef. Combine spaghetti sauce, tomato sauce, pepper and sugar. Stir in spinach, cottage cheese, eggs and Parmesan cheese. Add to ground beef and pasta. Gently combine. Place in freezer bag. Label and freeze. 6 servings.

To serve: Thaw. Place in greased baking dish. Stir. Place baking dish on a baking sheet. Bake uncovered for 45 minutes at 350°. Top with more shredded Parmesan cheese.

Spaghetti and Company

1 pound lean ground beef
1 pound hot Italian sausage
2 cups chopped onion
2 teaspoons minced garlic
5 (26-ounce) jars spaghetti sauce
1/4 cup sugar

Brown ground beef and sausage with onion and garlic. Remove from heat. Add spaghetti sauce and sugar. Prepare Italian dishes or divide into freezer bags or containers for spaghetti. Label and freeze. Makes about 20 cups of sauce.

To serve: Thaw. Heat until hot and bubbly. Serve over hot spaghetti noodles. Top with Parmesan cheese.

Why "and Company?" This sauce is great with other Italian dishes such as manicotti, lasagna, ravioli and pizza. Decide how much sauce you will need and make enough for all the Italian recipes you desire to make all at once.

Cheese Manicotti

1 (8-ounce) package manicotti
1 1/2 cups Ricotta cheese
2 cups cottage cheese
1/2 cup softened cream cheese
1/2 cup shredded fresh Parmesan cheese
1 1/2 cups shredded Mozzarella cheese
1 tablespoon dried parsley flakes
1 teaspoon salt
1/4 teaspoon pepper
3 cups spaghetti sauce

Do not cook manicotti. Combine Ricotta cheese, cottage cheese, cream cheese, Parmesan cheese, Mozzarella cheese, dried parsley flakes, salt and pepper. Mix well. Cover bottom of a greased foil baking pan with spaghetti sauce. Place filling into a quart freezer bag. Zip closed. Snip off corner. Squeeze filling into each uncooked manicotti. Arrange on spaghetti sauce in pan. Pour spaghetti sauce over all. Cover with extra heavy foil. Label and freeze. 8 servings.

To serve: Thaw. Bake covered for 45 minutes at 350°. Uncover, top with more Mozzarella cheese and bake an additional 5 minutes or until cheese melts.

 For spaghetti sauce, try recipes on pages 95, 119, or 161.

Chicken Stuffed Manicotti

3/4 pound boneless skinless chicken breast
1/4 cup minced onion
1/4 cup minced mushrooms
4 teaspoons butter
1/4 pound ground pork
3/4 cup cottage cheese
1/3 cup cream
1/2 teaspoon salt
1 dash pepper
1 (8-ounce) package manicotti
3 cups spaghetti sauce

Bake chicken breast, uncovered, for 20 minutes at 350°, until cooked through. Meanwhile, cook onion and mushrooms in butter until soft. Add ground pork and brown. Remove from heat. Finely chop chicken breast (in food processor) and add to ground pork. Stir in cottage cheese, cream, salt and pepper. Cover bottom of a greased foil baking pan with spaghetti sauce. Place filling into a quart freezer bag. Zip closed. Snip off corner. Squeeze filling into each uncooked manicotti. Arrange on spaghetti sauce in pan. Spoon spaghetti sauce over all. Cover with extra heavy foil. Label and freeze. 8 servings.

To serve: Thaw. Bake uncovered 45 minutes at 350°.

Delicious topped with cheese sauce: 1 cup cream, 1/4 cup butter, 1/4 cup shredded fresh Parmesan cheese, 1/4 cup shredded Jack cheese, 1/2 cup Mozzarella cheese. Heat until cheese melts.

Simply Lasagna

2 cups cottage cheese
1 egg, slightly beaten
1 tablespoon dried parsley flakes
2 tablespoons canned Parmesan cheese
1 cup shredded Mozzarella cheese
1 1/2 cups shredded Monterey Jack cheese
3 cups spaghetti sauce
12 lasagna noodles

Combine the cottage cheese, egg, parsley and Parmesan cheese. Cover bottom of a greased foil baking pan with spaghetti sauce. Layer uncooked noodles, sauce, half the Mozzarella and half the Jack cheese. Top with another layer of noodles, then all the cottage cheese mixture. Top with another layer of noodles, then the remaining Mozzarella and Jack cheeses and cover with a thick layer of spaghetti sauce. Cover with extra heavy foil. Label and freeze. 12 servings.

To serve: Thaw. Bake covered for 45 to 60 minutes at 375°. Uncover, top with more Mozzarella cheese and bake an additional 5 minutes or until cheese is melted.

 For spaghetti sauce, try recipes on pages 95, 119, or 161.

Italian Shells

1 (12-ounce) package uncooked shell pasta
1/4 cup melted butter
1 pound lean ground beef
1 cup chopped onion
1 cup sliced mushrooms
3 cups spaghetti sauce
1 cup cottage cheese
1/2 cup sour cream
1 (8-ounce) package softened cream cheese

Cook pasta in boiling, salted water for 2 minutes less than the shortest time recommended on package. Drain. Pour melted butter over pasta and mix. Brown ground beef with onion and mushrooms. Remove from heat and stir in spaghetti sauce. In a separate bowl, combine cottage cheese, sour cream and cream cheese. In greased foil baking pan, make the following layers: 1/2 the pasta, 1/2 the sauce, all the cheese mixture, the remaining pasta, the remaining sauce. Cover with extra heavy foil. Label and freeze. 8 servings.

To serve: Thaw. Bake covered for 1 hour at 350. Uncover and top with shredded Mozzarella cheese. Bake 10 minutes.

Creamed Corn and Beef

1 pound lean ground beef
1 cup chopped onion
1 (10.75-ounce) can tomato soup
1 1/2 cups water
2 cups uncooked elbow macaroni
1/2 teaspoon salt
1/4 teaspoon pepper
1 (15-ounce) can creamed corn
1 (10.75-ounce) can tomato soup
1 cup shredded Cheddar cheese

Brown ground beef with onion. Stir in 1 can tomato soup, water, uncooked macaroni, salt and pepper. Bring to boil. Immediately reduce heat to low and simmer barely 5 minutes. Do not overcook. Remove from heat and stir in creamed corn. (Do not add remaining tomato soup and Cheddar cheese until baking.) Allow to cool. Place in freezer bag. Label and freeze. 8 servings.

To serve: Thaw. Place in greased baking dish. Top with 1 can tomato soup. Cover and bake for 45 minutes at 350°. Uncover. Top with 1 cup shredded Cheddar cheese. Return to oven for an additional 15 minutes.

Beefy Macaroni

2 cups uncooked elbow macaroni
1 pound lean ground beef
1 cup chopped onion
2 (8-ounce) cans tomato sauce
1 teaspoon celery salt
1/4 teaspoon pepper
1/2 cup beef broth
1 (8-ounce) package softened cream cheese
1 cup cottage cheese
1/2 cup sour cream

Cook macaroni in boiling, salted water for 2 minutes less than the shortest time recommended on package. Drain. Brown ground beef with onion. Remove from heat. Add macaroni, tomato sauce, celery salt, pepper and broth. In a separate bowl, beat together cream cheese, cottage cheese and sour cream. In a greased foil baking pan, make 2 layers each of beef and pasta mixture then cheese mixture. Cover with extra heavy foil. Label and freeze. 8 servings.

To serve: Thaw. Bake covered for 1 hour at 350°.

 Substitute other interesting pasta shapes for the macaroni.

Beef Noodle Onion Bake

3 cups uncooked corkscrew pasta
1 pound lean ground beef
1/2 cup chopped green bell pepper
1 (14-ounce) can Italian tomatoes
1 (10.75-ounce) can cream of mushroom soup
1 cup shredded Cheddar cheese
1/4 teaspoon pepper
1 (6-ounce) can French fried onions

Cook pasta in boiling, salted water for 2 minutes less than the shortest time recommended on package. Drain. Brown ground beef with green bell pepper. Remove from heat. Add tomatoes, soup, cheese and pepper. Stir in pasta. Mix well. (Do not add onions until baking.) Place in freezer bag. Label and freeze. 6 servings.

To serve: Thaw. Stir. Place half in greased baking dish. Cover with half the French fried onions. Pour the remaining noodle mixture over top. Bake covered for 45 minutes at 350°. Uncover. Top with remaining onions. Bake an additional 10 minutes.

 Substitute other interesting pasta shapes for the corkscrew pasta.

Biscuit Beef Bake

1 pound lean ground beef
1/2 cup chopped onion
1 teaspoon minced garlic
1 (14.5-ounce) can diced tomatoes
1 (15-ounce) can pork and beans
1 (8-ounce) can tomato sauce
1/2 cup corn
2 teaspoons chili powder
1 teaspoon salt
1/2 teaspoon pepper
1 (7.5-ounce) can refrigerated biscuit dough

Brown ground beef with onion and garlic. Remove from heat. Stir in tomatoes, pork and beans, tomato sauce, corn, chili powder, salt and pepper. (Do not add biscuits until baking.) Place in freezer bag. Label and freeze. 6 servings.

To serve: Thaw. Place in greased baking dish. Bake uncovered at 400° for 30 minutes. Cut each biscuit in four pieces. Arrange on top of hot mixture. Return to oven and bake an additional 15 minutes.

Barbeque Beef and Biscuits

1 pound lean ground beef
1 cup chopped onion
1/2 cup chopped celery
1/2 cup chopped green bell pepper
1/2 teaspoon salt
dash of pepper
1 (10.75-ounce) can tomato soup
1/2 cup barbeque sauce
1 (7.5-ounce) can refrigerated biscuit dough

Brown ground beef with onion, celery and bell pepper. Season with salt and pepper. Remove from heat. Add tomato soup and barbeque sauce. Allow to cool. (Do not add biscuits until baking.) Place in freezer bag. Label and freeze. 6 servings.

To serve: Thaw. Pour into greased baking dish. Bake for 30 minutes at 400°. Cut each biscuit into four pieces and arrange on hot barbeque beef. Return to oven and bake an additional 15 minutes.

Cowboy Barbeque

1 pound ground beef
1 cup chopped onion
1 (15-ounce) can baked beans
1 cup barbeque sauce
2 tablespoons brown sugar
1 (7.5-ounce) can refrigerated biscuit dough
1 cup shredded Cheddar cheese

Brown ground beef with onion. Remove from heat. Stir in beans, barbeque sauce and brown sugar. (Do not add biscuits until baking.) Place in freezer bag. Label and freeze. 6 servings.

To serve: Thaw. Pour into round greased baking dish. Bake uncovered for 30 minutes at 400°. Cut refrigerator biscuits in half. Arrange upright (cut edge down) and slightly overlapping around edge of baking dish. Return to oven and bake 15 minutes. Top with cheese and bake 5 minutes more.

Meat Loaf and Potatoes

1 1/2 pounds very lean ground beef
3/4 cup evaporated milk
1/2 cup oatmeal
1/4 cup ketchup
1/4 cup chopped onion
1 teaspoon salt
1/4 teaspoon pepper
3 cups frozen cubed hash browns

Combine ground beef, evaporated milk, oatmeal, ketchup, onion, salt and pepper. Place frozen potatoes on bottom of a greased foil baking pan. Spread meat mixture on top of potatoes. Cover with extra heavy foil. Label and freeze. 6 servings.

To serve: Thaw. Bake uncovered at 350° for 45 minutes. Serve with ketchup.

To serve **Meat Loaf and Potatoes** with fresh sliced potatoes, mix the meat loaf and freeze in a freezer bag. Omit frozen hash brown potatoes.

To serve: Thaw. Spread meat loaf over 4 cups thinly sliced potatoes. Bake at 350° for 75 minutes. Serve with ketchup.

Pizza Meat Loaf

1 1/2 pounds very lean ground beef
1/2 cup cracker crumbs
1/4 cup chopped onion
1 egg, slightly beaten
1/2 cup shredded fresh Parmesan cheese
1 teaspoon salt
1/2 teaspoon oregano
1/2 cup evaporated milk
1/4 cup chopped green bell pepper
1 cup chopped mushrooms
1/2 cup spaghetti sauce
1 cup shredded Mozzarella cheese

Combine ground beef, cracker crumbs, onion, egg, Parmesan cheese, salt, oregano, evaporated milk, green pepper, mushrooms and spaghetti sauce. Place in freezer bag. Label and freeze. 6 servings.

To serve: Thaw. Place in greased loaf pan or shape into a loaf and place on a greased baking sheet. Bake at 350° for 45 minutes. Top with 1 cup Mozzarella cheese. Return to oven and bake 10 minutes longer.

For quick cracker crumbs, place crackers in a zippered plastic bag. Place bag on a flat surface. Roll a rolling pin over the crackers until crushed to the desired size.

Cheesy Meat Loaf

1 1/2 pounds very lean ground beef
2 cups fresh bread crumbs
1 cup tomato juice
1/2 cup chopped onion
2 eggs, slightly beaten
2 teaspoon beef bouillon
1/4 teaspoon pepper
6 slices American cheese

Combine ground beef, crumbs, tomato juice, onion, eggs, bouillon and pepper. Shape half of the meat mixture in a shallow loaf shape. Top with the cheese slices. Top with remaining meat mixture. Press edges together to seal cheese inside loaf. Place in freezer bag. Label and freeze. 6 servings.

To serve: Thaw. Place in greased loaf pan or shape into a loaf and place on a greased baking sheet. Bake for 1 hour at 350°. Top with additional cheese.

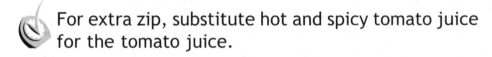 For extra zip, substitute hot and spicy tomato juice for the tomato juice.

To make fresh bread crumbs, pulse sliced bread in a food processor briefly until small crumbs form. 4 slices will make about 2 cups of fresh bread crumbs.

Onion Soup Meat Loaf

2 pounds very lean ground beef
6 crushed saltine crackers
1 (10.75-ounce) can onion soup
1/2 teaspoon salt
1/4 teaspoon pepper

Combine ground beef, crushed crackers, soup, salt and pepper. Place in freezer bag. Label and freeze. 8 servings.

To serve: Thaw. Place in greased loaf pan or shape into loaf and place on greased shallow baking dish. Bake for 1 hour at 350°.

To easily crush crackers, place crackers in a zippered plastic bag. Place bag on a flat surface. Roll a rolling pin over the crackers until crushed to the desired size.

Bacon Meat Loaf

2 pounds very lean ground beef
4 slices bacon, chopped
1 (.7-ounce) envelope Italian dressing mix
2 eggs, slightly beaten
1/3 cup finely chopped onion
1/2 cup fresh bread crumbs
4 slices bacon

Cook bacon until slightly crisp. Drain on paper towels. Combine ground beef, cooked bacon, Italian dressing mix, eggs, onion and bread crumbs. Mix well. Place in freezer bag. Label and freeze. 8 servings.

To serve: Thaw. Place in greased loaf pan or shape into a loaf and place on a greased shallow baking dish. Arrange 4 bacon slices on top. Bake for 1 hour at 350°.

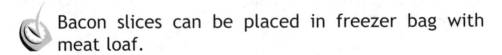

Bacon slices can be placed in freezer bag with meat loaf.

To make fresh bread crumbs, pulse a slice of bread in a food processor briefly until small crumbs form. One slice makes about 1/2 cup crumbs.

Glazed Meat Loaf

1/2 cup ketchup
1/3 cup packed brown sugar
1/4 cup lemon juice
1 teaspoon ground mustard
1 1/2 pounds very lean ground beef
1 1/2 cups fresh bread crumbs
1/4 cup chopped onion
1 egg, slightly beaten
1 teaspoon beef bouillon
1 teaspoon salt
1/4 teaspoon pepper

In a small bowl, combine ketchup, brown sugar, lemon juice and ground mustard. In large bowl, combine ground beef, bread crumbs, onion, egg, bouillon, salt and pepper. Mix well. Mix in 1/3 cup of the ketchup mixture. Place in freezer bag. Place remaining ketchup mixture in sandwich bag and place in freezer bag with meat loaf. Label and freeze. 6 servings.

To serve: Thaw. Place in greased loaf pan or shape into a loaf and place on greased baking pan. Bake 1 hour at 350°. Spread ketchup mixture on meat loaf and bake 10 minutes.

 To make fresh bread crumbs, see page 176.

 For quick lemon juice, see page 72.

Nacho Meat Loaf

1 cup thick tomato salsa
3/4 cup finely crushed nacho tortilla chips
1 egg
1 cup chopped onion
1 teaspoon minced garlic
1 (4-ounce) can diced green chiles
1 tablespoon chili powder
1 teaspoon salt
1/2 teaspoon cumin
1 1/2 pounds very lean ground beef
1/2 cup shredded sharp Cheddar cheese

Combine salsa, crushed tortilla chips, egg, onion, garlic, green chiles, chili powder, salt and cumin. Mix well. Add ground beef and mix until well combined. Place in freezer bag. Label and freeze. 6 servings.

To serve: Thaw. Place in greased loaf pan or shape into a loaf and place on shallow greased baking pan. Bake for 1 hour at 375°. Remove from oven and top with shredded sharp Cheddar cheese. Return to oven until cheese is melted.

 Cheese may be frozen in small bag in freezer bag with meat loaf.

Corny Meat Loaf

1 1/2 cups corn flakes, crushed
2 eggs
1 (8-ounce) can tomato sauce
1 cup chopped onion
1 cup chopped green bell pepper
1 cup frozen corn
1 1/2 teaspoons garlic salt
1/4 teaspoon pepper
2 pounds very lean ground beef
1/3 cup ketchup

Combine crushed corn flakes, eggs, tomato sauce, onion, bell pepper, corn, garlic salt and pepper. Mix well. Add ground beef. Mix well. Place in freezer bag. Label and freeze. 8 servings.

To serve: Thaw. Place in greased loaf pan or shape into a loaf and place on greased baking pan. Bake 45 minutes at 350°. Remove from oven and top with 1/3 cup ketchup. Return to oven and bake additional 15 minutes.

To easily crush corn flakes, place in a zippered plastic bag. Place bag on a flat surface. Roll a rolling pin over the corn flakes until crushed to the desired size.

California Dip Meat Loaf

1 (1.25-ounce) envelope onion soup mix
1 1/2 cups crushed potato chips
3/4 cup sour cream
2 eggs, slightly beaten
2 pounds very lean ground beef

Combine onion soup mix, crushed potato chips, sour cream and eggs. Add ground beef and mix well. Place in freezer bag. Label and freeze. 8 servings.

To serve: Thaw. Place in greased loaf pan or shape into a loaf and place on greased baking pan. Bake for 75 minutes at 375°.

 For extra flavor, substitute sour cream and onion flavored potato chips for the regular chips.

 To easily crush potato chips, place chips in a zippered plastic bag. Place bag on a flat surface. Roll a rolling pin over the potato chips until crushed to the desired size.

Very Best Meat Loaf

1 1/2 cups fresh bread crumbs
3/4 cup ketchup
1 (1.25-ounce) envelope onion soup mix
1/2 cup hot water
2 eggs
1 teaspoon Worcestershire sauce
1 pound ground beef
1/2 pound ground pork
1/2 pound ground veal
4 slices bacon
1 (8-ounce) can tomato sauce

Combine bread crumbs, ketchup, onion soup mix, hot water, eggs and Worcestershire sauce. Mix well. Add ground beef, pork and veal. Mix thoroughly. Place in freezer bag. Label and freeze. 8 servings.

To serve: Thaw. Shape into loaf and place on greased baking dish. Top with 4 slices of bacon. Pour 1 (8-ounce) can tomato sauce down middle of loaf. Smooth top to allow sauce to run down the sides. Bake for 75 minutes at 350°.

 To make fresh bread crumbs, pulse sliced bread in a food processor briefly until small crumbs form. 3 slices of bread will make about 1 1/2 cups of fresh bread crumbs.

 Bacon may be frozen with the meat loaf.

Stuffing Meat Loaves

1 (6-ounce) box stuffing mix
1 cup beef broth
2 eggs, slightly beaten
2 pounds very lean ground beef
1 (10.75-ounce) can beefy mushroom soup

Combine seasoning mix from stuffing with beef broth. Add stuffing and mix until completely moistened. Combine stuffing, eggs and ground beef. Mix well. Do not add beefy mushroom soup until baking. Place in freezer bag. Label and freeze. 8 servings.

To serve: Thaw. Shape into two oval loaves. Place side by side in greased shallow baking dish. Pour beefy mushroom soup over top of meat loaves. Bake uncovered for 45 minutes at 375°.

Basic Meatballs

1/2 pound lean ground beef
1/2 pound ground pork
1 egg, slightly beaten
1/2 teaspoon garlic salt
1 teaspoon salt
1/8 teaspoon pepper
1/2 cup dry bread crumbs
2 tablespoon minced onion
2 tablespoon Worcestershire sauce

Combine ground beef and pork. Mix in egg, garlic salt, salt, pepper, bread crumbs, onion and Worcestershire sauce. Shape into 1-inch meat balls. Use in desired recipe. To freeze meatballs for later use, arrange close together in a single layer on a foil-lined baking sheet. Bake in 350° oven for 7 minutes. Meatballs need not be cooked through. They will continue cooking when prepared in sauces. Freeze meatballs in single layer. Transfer to freezer bag. Label and freeze. 6 servings.

 See **Meatballs** section of Index for meatball sauce recipes.

Meatballs in Sour Cream Sauce

1 recipe **Basic Meatballs** (page 183)
1 cup sliced onion
1 tablespoon butter
1 (1-ounce) envelope brown gravy mix
1 (10.75-ounce) can cream of mushroom soup
1/2 cup sour cream

Shape 1-inch balls from meatball recipe. Brown on all sides or bake at 350° for 7 minutes. (Meatballs do not need to be cooked through.) Cook onion in butter until soft and golden. Make brown gravy according to envelope directions. Combine cooked onion, gravy, soup and sour cream. Add meatballs. Place in freezer bag. Label and freeze. 6 servings.

To serve: Thaw. Place in skillet and cook slowly for about 10 minutes. Cook and stir until sauce is smooth, basting meatballs often. Serve over hot buttered noodles.

Spaghetti and Meatballs

1 recipe **Basic Meatballs** (page 183)
1 (26-ounce) jar spaghetti sauce
1/2 cup chopped onion
2 cups sliced mushrooms
2 tablespoons butter
1 tablespoon sugar

Shape 3/4-inch balls from meatball recipe. Brown on all sides or bake at 350° for 7 minutes. (Meatballs do not need to be cooked through.) Cook onion and mushrooms in butter until soft and golden. Remove from heat. Stir in spaghetti sauce and sugar. Mix well. Add meatballs. Place in freezer bag. Label and freeze. 6 servings.

To serve: Thaw. Pour into skillet and simmer 15 minutes. Serve over hot spaghetti.

Cheesy Lasagna

1 pound lean ground beef
1 cup chopped onion
1/3 cup chopped green bell pepper
1 cup sliced mushrooms
1 (26-ounce) jar spaghetti sauce
1 tablespoon sugar
1 cup cottage cheese
1 (8-ounce) package softened cream cheese
1/4 cup sour cream
2 cups shredded Mozzarella cheese
12 uncooked lasagna noodles

Brown ground beef with onion, bell pepper and mush-rooms. Stir in spaghetti sauce and sugar. In a separate bowl, combine cottage cheese, cream cheese and sour cream. In a greased foil baking pan, make the following layers: sauce, uncooked noodles, sauce, half the Mozzarella cheese, uncooked noodles, all the cottage cheese mixture, uncooked noodles, remaining Mozzarella cheese and remaining sauce. Cover with extra heavy foil. Label and freeze. 12 servings.

To serve: Thaw. Bake covered 1 hour at 350°. Uncover and top with more Mozzarella cheese. Bake 5 minutes.

Mexican Lasagna

1 pound lean ground beef
1 cup chopped onion
1 (1.25-ounce) envelope taco seasoning
1/2 cup water
12 uncooked lasagna noodles
2 cups shredded Monterey Jack cheese
1 (16-ounce) can refried beans
1 cup sour cream
1 (2.25-ounce) can sliced black olives
1 1/4 cups water
1 1/4 cups salsa

Brown ground beef with onion. Add taco seasoning and water. Simmer 5 minutes. In a greased foil baking pan, make the following layers: uncooked noodles, half the beef mixture, half the cheese, uncooked noodles, refried beans, sour cream, drained olives, uncooked noodles, remaining cheese, remaining beef mixture. Combine water and salsa. Pour over all. Cover with extra heavy foil. Label and freeze. 12 servings.

To serve: Thaw. Bake covered for 1 hour at 350°. Uncover and top with additional Monterey Jack cheese.

Beefy Chinese Rice

1 pound lean ground beef
2 cups chopped onion
1 1/2 cups sliced celery
1 1/2 cups sliced mushrooms
1 (8-ounce) can sliced water chestnuts, drained
1 (10.75-ounce) can cream of mushroom soup
1 (10.75-ounce) can cream of chicken soup
1 1/2 cups chicken broth
1/4 cup soy sauce
1/4 teaspoon pepper
1/2 cup uncooked rice
1 1/2 cups chow mein noodles

Brown ground beef. Remove from heat. Add onion, celery, mushrooms and water chestnuts. Whisk together soups, broth, soy sauce and pepper. Stir in uncooked rice. Combine with meat and vegetables. (Do not add chow mein noodles until baking.) Place in freezer bag. Label and freeze. 6 servings.

To serve: Thaw. Place in greased baking dish. Stir well. Cover and bake for 45 minutes at 350°. Uncover and bake 15 minutes longer. Remove from oven and top with chow mein noodles. Bake an additional 10 minutes.

Beef and Cheese Roll-Ups

1 1/2 cups Ricotta cheese
1/4 cup shredded fresh Parmesan cheese
1 cup shredded Mozzarella cheese
1 egg, slightly beaten
1/4 teaspoon oregano
1/4 teaspoon garlic powder
2 cups spaghetti sauce
1 pound thin sliced deli roast beef
1/2 cup French fried onions

Combine Ricotta, Parmesan, Mozzarella, egg, oregano and garlic powder. Spoon spaghetti sauce over bottom of greased foil baking pan. Divide cheese mixture among the deli beef slices. Sprinkle with French fried onions. Roll up beef around cheese and place, seam side down, in pan on top of spaghetti sauce. Pour remaining spaghetti sauce over beef rolls. Cover with extra heavy foil. Label and freeze. 8 servings.

To serve: Thaw. Bake covered for 1 hour at 375°. Uncover and top with more Mozzarella cheese and French fried onions. Bake an additional 10 minutes.

 If beef slices are too small, combine 2 slices to make a larger roll-up.

Chili Beef and Rice

3/4 cup uncooked rice
1 3/4 cups beef broth
1 (6-ounce) can tomato paste
1 (1.25-ounce) envelope taco seasoning
1 cup beef broth
1 pound lean ground beef
1 cup chopped onion
2 cups frozen corn

Cook rice in beef broth according to rice package directions. Combine tomato paste, taco seasoning and 1 cup
beef broth. Brown ground beef with onion. In a greased
foil baking pan, make the following layers: half the
rice, half the corn, half the beef mixture and half the
sauce. Repeat layers with the remainder of each, ending with the remaining sauce. Cover with extra heavy
foil. Label and freeze. 8 servings.

To serve: Thaw. Bake covered for 1 hour at 375°. Serve
with corn chips and sour cream.

Steak and Vegetable Pie

1 pound beef sirloin steak
1 cup chopped onion
2 tablespoons canola oil
1 cup beef broth
1 (10.75-ounce) can beefy mushroom soup
1 tablespoon sugar
1/4 cup cold water
2 tablespoons cornstarch
1 (16-ounce) bag frozen mixed vegetables
pastry for 2 crust pie

Cut steak in 1/2-inch cubes. Brown steak in oil with onion over medium-high heat. Stir in broth, soup and sugar. Stir until smooth. Dissolve cornstarch in cold water. Stir into beef. Cook and stir until thick and bubbly. Remove from heat. Stir in mixed vegetables. Allow to cool. Pour into pie crust. Top with crust. Crimp edges. Cover with extra heavy foil. Label and freeze. 6 servings.

To serve: Thaw. Cut slits in top crust. Bake for 1 hour at 375°.

Beef and Broccoli

3/4 cup uncooked rice
1 pound lean ground beef
1 cup chopped onion
1 teaspoon minced garlic
1 (10-ounce) box frozen broccoli
1 (10.75-ounce) can cream of mushroom soup
1/2 cup beef broth
1 tablespoon Worcestershire sauce
1 teaspoon Italian seasoning
1 cup shredded Mozzarella cheese
1 cup French fried onions

Cook rice according to package directions. Brown ground beef with onion and garlic. Thaw broccoli and squeeze out water. Combine beef and broccoli. Stir in cooked rice, soup, broth, Worcestershire sauce, Italian seasoning and cheese. (Do not add onions until baking.) Place in freezer bag. Label and freeze. 6 servings.

To serve: Thaw. Place in greased baking dish. Bake uncovered for 35 minutes at 375°. Top with 1 cup French fried onions and bake an additional 10 minutes.

Pizza in a Dish

2 cups uncooked elbow macaroni
1 pound lean ground beef
1 cup chopped onion
1 cup chopped green bell pepper
1 teaspoon minced garlic
1 1/2 cups sliced mushrooms
2 cups spaghetti sauce
1 (4-ounce) package sliced pepperoni
1 (2.25-ounce) can sliced black olives
1/2 teaspoon oregano
1/2 teaspoon basil
1 tablespoon sugar
1/2 teaspoon salt
1/8 teaspoon pepper
1 1/2 cups shredded Mozzarella cheese

Cook macaroni in boiling, salted water for 2 minutes less than the shortest recommended time on package. Drain. Brown ground beef with onion, bell pepper, garlic and mushrooms. Remove from heat. Add spaghetti sauce, pepperoni, drained black olives, oregano, basil, sugar, salt and pepper. Stir in cooked macaroni. Place in freezer bag. Label and freeze. 8 servings.

To serve: Thaw. Place in greased baking dish. Bake covered for 45 minutes at 350°. Uncover, top with Mozzarella cheese and bake 5 minutes longer.

 Substitute any shape pasta for the elbow macaroni.

Ground Beef Stroganoff

2 cups sliced mushrooms
2 tablespoons butter
1 pound lean ground beef
1 cup chopped onion
1 (10.75-ounce) can cream of mushroom soup
1/8 teaspoon pepper
1/2 teaspoon salt
1 tablespoon sugar
1 cup sour cream

Cook mushrooms in butter for 5 minutes. Remove from pan. Brown ground beef with onion. Remove from heat. Return mushrooms to pan. Stir in soup, pepper, salt, sugar and sour cream. Place in freezer bag. Label and freeze. 6 servings.

To serve: Thaw. Heat and stir until smooth and hot throughout. Thin with a little milk, if necessary. Serve over hot buttered noodles.

Mock Filet Mignon

1 cup uncooked rice
1 1/2 pounds very lean ground beef
1 cup chopped onion
1 teaspoon minced garlic
1 1/2 teaspoon salt
1/4 teaspoon pepper
2 tablespoon Worcestershire sauce
1 tablespoon sugar
6 slices bacon

Cook rice according to package directions. Combine ground beef, cooked rice, onion, garlic, salt, pepper, Worcestershire sauce and sugar. Shape into 6 patties. Wrap a bacon strip around each. Place on a baking sheet and cover loosely with plastic wrap. Place in freezer just until patties are frozen. Place patties in freezer bag. Label and freeze. 6 servings.

To serve: Thaw. Grill for about 10 minutes each side, until cooked through. Or bake for 20 minutes at 375°. Serve like steak with baked potatoes and salad.

Corkscrew Chicken

3 cups uncooked corkscrew pasta
1 1/2 pounds boneless skinless chicken breast
1 cup chopped onion
3 tablespoons olive oil
1 teaspoon minced garlic
1 (26-ounce) jar spaghetti sauce
1 cup chicken broth

Cook corkscrew pasta in salted, boiling water for 2 minutes less than the shortest time recommended on package. Cut chicken into bite-sized pieces. Cook in olive oil with onion and garlic until no longer pink. Stir in spaghetti sauce and chicken broth. Remove from heat. Stir in cooked pasta. Allow to cool. Place in freezer bag. Label and freeze. 8 servings.

To serve: Thaw. Place in saucepan and heat until hot throughout. Serve with shredded fresh Parmesan cheese and garlic toast.

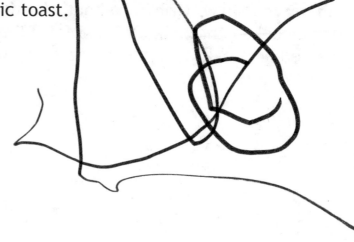

Navajo Tacos

1 (16-ounce) can refried beans
1/4 cup water
2 cups chicken broth
1/3 cup flour
1/2 cup butter
1 (4-ounce) can diced green chiles
1 (10-ounce) can tomatoes with chiles
10 flour tortillas
2 cups shredded Cheddar cheese
4 cups cooked, chopped chicken

Heat refried beans and mix with water to make spread-able, set aside. In a saucepan, combine chicken broth and flour. Add butter, green chiles and tomatoes with chiles. Heat until butter is melted and continue cooking until sauce is thick and bubbly. In a greased foil baking pan, make the following layers using half for each layer: torn tortillas, refried beans, cheese, chicken and sauce. Repeat layers using remainder of all ingredients. Cover with extra heavy foil. Label and freeze. 12 servings.

To serve: Thaw. Bake for 1 hour at 350°. Top with cheese. Serve with lettuce, sour cream and salsa.

Chicken and Broccoli

1 (16-ounce) bag frozen broccoli
1 (10.75-ounce) can cream of chicken soup
1 (10.75-ounce) can cream of mushroom soup
1/2 cup evaporated milk
1 cup mayonnaise
1 tablespoon lemon juice
dash of pepper
3 cups cooked, chopped chicken
1 cup French fried onions

Thaw and squeeze water from broccoli. In a large bowl, combine broccoli, chicken soup, mushroom soup, evaporated milk, mayonnaise, lemon juice and pepper. Stir in chicken. (Do not add onions until baking.) Place in freezer bag. Label and freeze. 6 servings.

To serve: Thaw. Place in greased baking dish. Bake covered for 1 hour at 350°. Uncover. Top with 1 cup French fried onions and bake 10 minutes longer.

Broccoli Chicken and Rice

1 cup uncooked rice
1 (10-ounce) package frozen broccoli
1 cup chopped onion
1 (10.75-ounce) can cream of chicken soup
1/2 cup sour cream
1/2 cup chicken broth
1/2 cup mayonnaise
1 1/2 cup shredded Monterey Jack cheese
3 cups cooked, chopped chicken
1 cup French fried onions

Cook rice according to package directions. Thaw and squeeze water from broccoli. In a large bowl, combine broccoli, onion, soup, sour cream, chicken broth and mayonnaise. Mix well. Stir in cheese, cooked rice and chicken. Place in freezer bag. Label and freeze. 6 servings.

To serve: Thaw. Place in greased baking dish. Bake covered for hour at 350°. Uncover and top with French fried onions. Bake additional 10 minutes.

Green Chile Chicken Soup

4 cups chicken broth
3 cups cooked, chopped chicken
1 (16-ounce) bag frozen corn
1/2 teaspoon cumin
1 teaspoon minced garlic
2 teaspoons chicken bouillon granules
1 (4-ounce) can diced green chiles
1 cup cream
1 teaspoon salt
1/4 teaspoon pepper

In a large bowl, combine chicken broth, chicken, corn, cumin, garlic, bouillon, green chiles, cream, salt and pepper. Place in freezer bag or container. Label and freeze. 6 servings.

To serve: Thaw. Heat just to boiling. Serve with sour cream, salsa and corn chips or tortilla chips.

Chicken and Dressing

2 cups chicken broth
1/2 cup melted butter
1 (8-ounce) box chicken stuffing
1 cup sour cream
1 (10.75-ounce) can cream of mushroom soup
4 cups cooked, chopped chicken

Combine chicken broth and butter. Stir in stuffing and seasoning mix from stuffing. Combine sour cream and soup. Stir into stuffing. Add chicken. Place in freezer bag. Label and freeze. 8 servings.

To serve: Thaw. Place in greased baking dish. Bake covered for 30 minutes at 350°. Uncover and bake 20 minutes longer.

Cheesy Chicken and Rice

1 1/2 cups uncooked rice
2 (10.75-ounce) cans cream of chicken soup
1 cup evaporated milk
1 cup shredded Monterey Jack cheese
dash of pepper
2 pounds boneless skinless chicken breast
1 teaspoon rotisserie chicken seasoning

Cook rice according to package directions. Mix soup, milk, cheese, cooked rice and pepper. Place in greased foil baking pan. Top with chicken pieces. Sprinkle with rotisserie chicken seasoning. Cover with extra heavy foil. Label and freeze. 6 servings.

To serve: Thaw. Bake covered for 40 minutes at 350°. Uncover and bake 20 minutes longer. Stir before serving.

Chicken and Biscuits

1 (10.75-ounce) can cream of chicken soup
3/4 cup evaporated milk
5 slices American cheese
1 (10-ounce) frozen peas and carrots
3 cups cooked, chopped chicken
1 (7.5-ounce) can refrigerated biscuit dough

Combine soup, milk and cheese. Cook gently until cheese melts. Remove from heat. Stir in peas and carrots and chicken. Allow to cool. (Do not add biscuits.) Place in freezer bag. Label and freeze. 6 servings.

To serve: Thaw. Heat until hot and bubbly. Serve over biscuits.

For an alternate serving option, thaw and pour into a greased baking dish. Bake uncovered for 30 minutes at 400°. Cut biscuits in fourths and place on hot chicken. Return to oven and bake for an additional 15 minutes.

Chicken and Rice

1 1/2 cups uncooked rice
1 1/2 cups baby carrots
1 (10.75-ounce) can cream of chicken soup
1 (10.75-ounce) can cream of mushroom soup
1 (10.75-ounce) can cream of celery soup
1/2 cup evaporated milk
2 pounds boneless skinless chicken breast
3 tablespoons melted butter

Cook rice according to package directions. Boil carrots in salted water for 2 minutes. Drain. Mix soups, milk and cooked rice. Add carrots. Place in greased foil baking pan. Arrange chicken pieces on top. Brush with melted butter. Cover with extra heavy foil. Label and freeze. 6 servings.

To serve: Thaw. Bake covered for 40 minutes at 350°. Uncover and bake 20 minutes longer.

Turkey Dressing Pie

1 (8-ounce) box turkey stuffing mix
1/2 cup chicken broth
2 tablespoons melted butter
1 egg, slightly beaten
1 cup chopped onion
3 tablespoons butter
1 1/2 cups turkey gravy
1 teaspoon Worcestershire sauce
1 cup frozen peas and carrots
3 cups cooked, chopped turkey

Combine dressing, seasoning packet, chicken broth, melted butter and egg. Press onto bottom and sides of a greased foil pie pan. Cook and stir onion in butter until soft. Remove from heat. Stir in turkey gravy, Worcestershire sauce, peas and carrots and turkey. Pour into dressing crust. Cover tightly with extra heavy foil. Label and freeze. 6 servings.

To serve: Thaw. Bake uncovered for 45 minutes at 375°.

 For turkey gravy, use leftover gravy, make gravy from a mix, or use a jar of purchased gravy.

 Try adding 1/3 cup sweetened, dried cranberries to the stuffing crust. Delicious!

Mayonnaise Chicken

1 (6.9-ounce) box chicken rice and pasta mix
2 (10.75-ounce) cans cream of chicken soup
1 cup sour cream
1 cup mayonnaise
4 cups cooked, chopped chicken
2 cups shredded Monterey Jack cheese

Prepare rice and pasta mix according to box directions. Combine soup, sour cream and mayonnaise. Stir together rice, soup mixture, chicken and cheese. Place in freezer bag. Label and freeze. 8 servings.

To serve: Thaw. Place in greased baking dish. Bake covered for 45 minutes at 350°. Uncover and top with shredded Jack cheese. Return to oven for 5 minutes or until cheese melts.

Country Chicken and Vegetables

1 (10.75-ounce) can cream of chicken soup
1 (10.75-ounce) can cream of mushroom soup
1 (16-ounce) bag frozen mixed vegetables
1 (24-ounce) bag frozen shredded hash browns
3 cups cooked, chopped chicken
2 cups French fried onions

Combine soups. Do not thaw vegetables or potatoes. Stir in vegetables, hash browns and chicken. (Do not add onions until baking.) Place in freezer bag. Label and freeze. 12 servings.

To serve: Thaw. Place in greased baking dish. Add 1 cup French fried onions. Bake uncovered for 45 minutes at 350°. Top with remaining 1 cup French fried onions. Return to oven and bake 10 additional minutes.

There are many different combinations of frozen mixed vegetables available. For variety, substitute any combination.

Tortilla Chicken

1 (10.75-ounce) can cream of chicken soup
1 (10.75-ounce) can cream of mushroom soup
1 cup chopped onion
1 (4-ounce) can diced green chiles
2 cups sour cream
12 corn tortillas
1 cup canola oil
4 cups cooked, chopped chicken
1 cup shredded Monterey Jack cheese
1 cup shredded Cheddar cheese

Combine soups, onion, green chiles and sour cream. Heat 1 cup oil in large skillet. Cook tortillas briefly, one at a time, for about 20 seconds on each side. Drain on paper towels. Cut tortillas into fourths. In a greased foil baking pan, make the following layers, using half for both layers: tortillas, chicken, cheese, sauce. Repeat layers. Cover with extra heavy foil. Label and freeze. 12 servings.

To serve: Thaw. Bake covered for 60 minutes at 350°. Uncover. Top with more shredded Cheddar cheese. Bake 10 minutes. Serve with shredded lettuce, sour cream, diced tomatoes, sliced olives and salsa.

 Corn tortillas will turn mushy and fall apart if they are not cooked before freezing in this recipe.

Chicken Enchiladas

1/2 cup chopped onion
2 tablespoons butter
1 (4-ounce) can diced green chiles
3 cups cooked, chopped chicken
1 (12-ounce) can evaporated milk
1 (10.75-ounce) can cream of chicken soup
1 1/2 cups sour cream
2 cups shredded Monterey Jack cheese
10 flour tortillas

Cook onion in butter until soft. Remove from heat. Stir in green chiles and chicken. In a bowl, combine evaporated milk, soup and sour cream. Dip tortillas, one at a time, in sauce. Place 3 tablespoons chicken mixture down center of each tortilla. Sprinkle with cheese. Roll up. Place seam down in greased foil baking pan. Repeat with remaining tortillas. Top with remaining sauce. Cover with extra heavy foil. Label and freeze. 10 servings.

To serve: Thaw. Bake covered 60 minutes at 350°.

Ham and Chicken Roll-Ups

1 cup uncooked rice
1/4 cup minced onion
1/4 cup minced celery
1/4 cup chopped mushrooms
3 tablespoons butter
1 1/2 cups cooked, chopped chicken
1 (10.75-ounce) can cream of chicken soup
6 slices cooked ham
1/2 cup sour cream
1/4 cup milk
1/4 teaspoon pepper
1 cup shredded Swiss cheese
1 cup French fried onions

Cook rice according to package directions. Arrange cooked rice on bottom of greased foil baking pan. Cook onion, celery and mushrooms in butter until soft. Combine chicken, 1/3 cup soup, onion, celery and mushrooms. Divide among the 6 slices of ham. Roll up and place seam side down on top of rice. Combine sour cream, milk, pepper and remaining soup. Pour over roll-ups. Cover with extra heavy foil. Label and freeze. 6 servings.

To serve: Thaw. Bake uncovered for 45 minutes at 350°. Top with cheese and French fried onions. Bake 10 minutes longer.

Chicken and Ham Dinner

2 (10.75-ounce) cans cream of chicken soup
3/4 cup mayonnaise
1/2 cup evaporated milk
3 tablespoons honey
2 tablespoons Dijon mustard
2 cups cooked, chopped chicken
2 cups chopped ham
1 (24-ounce) bag frozen shredded hash browns
1 (16-ounce) bag frozen green beans, corn, sliced carrots

In large bowl combine soup, mayonnaise, milk, honey and mustard. Stir in ham and chicken. (Do not thaw potatoes or vegetables.) Add hash brown potatoes and vegetables. Place in freezer bag. Label and freeze. 12 servings.

To serve: Thaw. Place in greased baking dish. Bake covered for 1 hour at 350°. Uncover and top with French fried onions and return to oven. Bake an additional 10 minutes.

Substitute any combination of frozen mixed vegetables for frozen green beans, corn and sliced carrots.

Creamy Chicken and Pasta

3 cups uncooked wide noodles
1 (10.75-ounce) can cream of chicken soup
1 (12-ounce) can evaporated milk
1/3 cup shredded fresh Parmesan cheese
1 cup shredded Mozzarella cheese
3 cups cooked, chopped chicken
1 (6-ounce) can French fried onions

Cook noodles in boiling, salted water for 2 minutes less than the shortest time recommended on package. Drain. Combine soup, milk and cheeses. Stir in chicken and pasta. (Do not add onions until baking.) Place in freezer bag. Label and freeze. 6 servings.

To serve: Thaw. Place in greased baking dish. Stir in half the can of French fried onions. Bake covered for 45 minutes at 350°. Uncover and top with remaining French fried onions. Bake an additional 10 minutes.

 Substitute any shape pasta for the wide noodles.

Turkey and Stuffing Roll-Ups

1 (6-ounce) package turkey stuffing mix
1 (10.75-ounce) can cream of chicken soup
3/4 cup milk
1 pound sliced smoked turkey
2 cups French fried onions

Prepare stuffing according to package directions but do not bake. Combine soup and milk. Spoon 1/4 cup stuffing on each smoked turkey slice. Sprinkle with French fried onions. Roll up and place seam side down in greased foil baking pan. Pour soup mixture over all. Cover with extra heavy foil. Label and freeze. 6 servings.

To serve: Thaw. Bake uncovered for 40 minutes at 350°. Top with additional French fried onions. Bake 5 minutes longer.

For Chicken and Stuffing Roll-Ups, substitute chicken stuffing mix and sliced deli chicken for the turkey stuffing and sliced smoked turkey.

Ham Loaf with Pineapple Sauce

1 (8-ounce) can pineapple tidbits
1 teaspoon cornstarch
1 tablespoon apple cider vinegar
1/4 cup chicken broth
2 tablespoons brown sugar
1 teaspoon ketchup
1/2 pound coarsely chopped ham
1 pound ground pork
1 1/2 cups fresh bread crumbs
1/2 cup milk
2 eggs
2 teaspoons ground mustard
1/4 teaspoon pepper

Drain pineapple and reserve syrup. In a small saucepan, combine cornstarch, vinegar, broth, brown sugar, ketchup and 1/4 cup reserved pineapple syrup. Cook and stir until thick and bubbly. Add pineapple. Place ham in food processor and pulse until finely chopped. Combine ham and ground pork and kneed with your hands until well mixed. In another bowl, combine crumbs, milk, eggs, ground mustard and pepper. Add 1/4 cup of the pineapple sauce. Mix well. Add to the meat and mix well. Place in freezer bag. Place remaining pineapple sauce in small bag and place in bag with meat loaf. Label and freeze. 6 servings.

To serve: Thaw. Place in greased loaf pan. Bake for 75 minutes at 350°. Heat pineapple sauce until hot and bubbly. Serve sauce with meat loaf.

Pork Loaf with Applesauce Glaze

1 tablespoon butter
1 cup finely chopped onion
1 cup fresh bread crumbs
1 cup applesauce
1 egg
3/4 teaspoon salt
1/4 teaspoon pepper
1 1/2 pounds ground pork
1 teaspoon Dijon mustard
1/2 cup applesauce

Cook onion in butter until soft. Combine softened onion, bread crumbs, 1 cup applesauce, egg, salt and pepper. Add ground pork and mix well. Place in freezer bag. Combine mustard and 1/2 cup applesauce. Place in small bag and place in freezer bag with meat loaf. Label and freeze. 6 servings.

To serve: Thaw. Place meat in greased loaf pan. Spread applesauce mustard mixture over top. Cover with foil. Place loaf pan on baking sheet and bake for 30 minutes at 375°. Remove foil and bake 30 minutes.

Ham and Noodles

2 cups uncooked wide noodles
2 tablespoons butter
2 tablespoons flour
1 cup milk
1 cup shredded American cheese
1/2 teaspoon salt
2 cups cubed ham
1 cup frozen petite peas

Cook noodles in boiling, salted water for 2 minutes less than the shortest time recommended on package. Drain. Melt butter and stir in flour. Cook and stir until bubbly but not brown. Stir in milk. Continue to cook and stir until thick and bubbly. Remove from heat and stir in cheese and salt. Stir until melted. Add ham, noodles and peas. Place in freezer bag. Label and freeze. 6 servings.

To serve: Thaw. Place in greased baking dish. Bake covered for 45 minutes at 350°. Uncover. Top with buttered bread crumbs. Bake for 10 minutes.

To make buttered bread crumbs, melt 1/4 cup butter in glass dish in microwave. Stir in 1 cup dry bread crumbs. Cracker crumbs may be substituted.

Cheesy Ham and Potatoes

1 (8-ounce) package cream cheese
2 (10.75-ounce) cans cream of celery soup
1/2 cup minced onion
1 1/2 cups cubed ham
1 1/2 cups shredded Monterey Jack cheese
1/4 teaspoon pepper
1 (24-ounce) bag frozen shredded hash browns

Soften cream cheese and combine with soup. Stir in onions, ham, Jack cheese and pepper. Break apart hash browns (do not thaw). Gently stir into cheese mixture. Place in freezer bag. Label and freeze. 12 servings.

To serve: Thaw. Place in greased baking dish. Bake covered for 1 hour at 350°. Uncover and top with shredded Cheddar cheese. Return to oven until cheese is melted.

Ham and Potato Scallop

1 (4.9-ounce) box scalloped potato mix
2 cups boiling water
2 tablespoons butter
3/4 cup milk
2 cups cubed ham
1 (12-ounce) bag frozen French green beans
1 cup shredded Cheddar cheese

Stir sauce mix from scalloped potato package into boiling water with butter. Pour over potatoes. Stir in milk, ham, green beans and cheese. Place in freezer bag. Label and freeze. 6 servings.

To serve: Thaw. Place in greased baking dish. Bake uncovered for 35 minutes at 400°. Uncover and top with more shredded Cheddar cheese. Return to oven until cheese melts.

Swiss Ham and Noodles

3 cups uncooked wide noodles
1 cup chopped onion
1/2 cup chopped green bell pepper
1/2 cup sliced mushrooms
3 tablespoons butter
1 (10.75-ounce) can cream of mushroom soup
1 cup sour cream
2 cups cubed ham
2 cups shredded Swiss cheese

Cook noodles in boiling, salted water for 2 minutes less than shortest time recommended on package. Drain. Cook onion, bell pepper and mushrooms in butter until soft and liquid is gone. Stir in soup and sour cream. Whisk until smooth. In a greased foil baking pan, make the following layers, using half for each layer: noodles, ham, cheese, sauce. Repeat layers ending with the remaining sauce. Cover with extra heavy foil. Label and freeze. 6 servings.

To serve: Thaw. Bake covered for 1 hour at 350°. Uncover. Top with additional shredded Swiss cheese. Bake 5 minutes.

Cheesy Ham and Noodles

3 cups uncooked corkscrew pasta
2 cups cubed ham
1 cup shredded American cheese
1 cup shredded Mozzarella cheese
1 (10.75-ounce) can cream of celery soup
1 cup sour cream

Cook noodles in boiling, salted water for 2 minutes less than the shortest time recommended on package. Drain. Combine cheeses, soup and sour cream. Stir in ham and noodles. Place in freezer bag. Label and freeze. 6 servings.

To serve: Thaw. Place in greased baking dish. Bake covered for 45 minutes at 350°. Stir before serving.

 Substitute any interesting pasta shape for the corkscrew pasta.

Ham Primavera

1 (8-ounce) package uncooked thin spaghetti
1 cup sliced mushrooms
1 cup chopped onion
2 tablespoons butter
2 tablespoons flour
2 teaspoons chicken bouillon
1/2 teaspoon salt
1/8 teaspoon pepper
2 cups milk
2 cups cubed ham
1 (10-ounce) package frozen petite peas

Cook spaghetti in boiling, salted water for 2 minutes less than shortest time recommended on package. Drain. Cook mushrooms and onion in butter until soft. Stir in flour, bouillon, salt and pepper. Gently stir in milk. Cook and stir until thick and bubbly. Remove from heat. Stir in ham, peas and spaghetti. Allow to cool. Place in freezer bag. Label and freeze. 8 servings.

To serve: Thaw. Heat until hot throughout. Serve with garlic toast.

Frozen petite peas are younger, smaller and much more tender than regular peas. They are usually found right next to the regular frozen peas.

Pork Chops and Potatoes

6 pork chops
1 teaspoon seasoned salt
1 tablespoon canola oil
1 (10.75-ounce) can cream of celery soup
2/3 cup evaporated milk
1 cup sour cream
1/2 teaspoon salt
1/8 teaspoon pepper
1 cup shredded Monterey Jack cheese
2/3 cup French fried onions
3 cups frozen shredded hashbrowns
1 cup French fried onions

Sprinkle pork chops with seasoned salt and brown in oil on both sides. Combine soup, milk and sour cream until smooth. Add salt, pepper, cheese and 2/3 cup onions. Mix in hash brown potatoes (do not thaw). Place in greased foil baking pan. Arrange chops on top of potatoes. Press down. (Do not add remaining French fried onions until baking.) Cover with extra heavy foil. Label and freeze. 6 servings.

To serve: Thaw. Bake covered for 1 hour at 350°. Uncover and top with French fried onions. Return to oven and bake an additional 10 minutes.

Scalloped Pork Chops

6 pork chops
1 teaspoon salt
1 tablespoon canola oil
1 (4.9-ounce) box scalloped potato mix
2 cups boiling water
2 tablespoons butter
1 (10.75-ounce) can cream of chicken soup
2/3 cup milk
1 teaspoon Worcestershire sauce
1 cup frozen mixed vegetables

Sprinkle chops with salt and brown in oil on both sides. Stir sauce mix from potatoes into boiling water. Add butter and stir until melted. Add potatoes. Mix together soup, milk and Worcestershire sauce. Add to potatoes. Stir in mixed vegetables. Place in greased foil baking pan. Arrange chops on top of potatoes. Cover with extra heavy foil. Label and freeze. 6 servings.

To serve: Thaw. Bake covered for 1 hour at 350°. Uncover and bake 20 minutes.

Tuna Bow Ties

3 cups uncooked bow tie pasta
1 (10.75-ounce) can cream of chicken soup
1 (12-ounce) can evaporated milk
1/4 cup chopped onion
1/2 cup shredded American cheese
1/2 cup shredded Monterey Jack cheese
1 (6-ounce) can tuna, drained
1 cup frozen petite peas

Cook pasta in boiling, salted water for 2 minutes less than the shortest time recommended on package. Mix together soup, milk and onion. Stir in cheeses, tuna, peas and bow ties. Place in freezer bag. Label and freeze. 6 servings.

To serve: Thaw. Bake covered in greased baking dish for 40 minutes at 350°. Uncover. Top with buttered cracker crumbs and bake 10 minutes.

 For buttered cracker crumbs, melt 2 tablespoons butter. Stir in 1/2 cup finely crushed butter crackers.

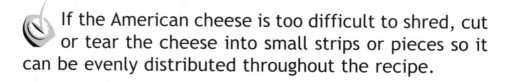 If the American cheese is too difficult to shred, cut or tear the cheese into small strips or pieces so it can be evenly distributed throughout the recipe.

 For **Chicken Bow Ties**, substitute 1 cup cooked, chopped chicken for the tuna.

Tuna Fettuccine

1/2 cup chopped onion
2 tablespoons butter
1 cup cream
1 (10.75-ounce) can cream of mushroom soup
1 (10.75-ounce) can cream of chicken soup
1 tablespoon sugar
6 slices American cheese
1 (6-ounce) can tuna, drained
1 (12-ounce) package fettuccine

Cook onion in butter until soft. Add cream, soups and sugar. Whisk until smooth. Arrange cheese slices on top of sauce and allow to melt. Whisk until smooth. Stir in tuna. Allow to cool. (Do not add fettuccine noodles until serving.) Place in freezer bag. Label and freeze. 6 servings.

To serve: Thaw. Heat and stir until smooth and bubbly. Serve over hot fettuccine noodles.

 For **Chicken Fettuccine**, substitute 1 cup cooked, chopped chicken for the tuna.

Tuna Stroganoff

3/4 cup sliced mushrooms
2 tablespoons butter
1 (10.75-ounce) cream of chicken mushroom soup
3/4 cup sour cream
1/2 cup mayonnaise
3/4 cup evaporated milk
1/2 teaspoon salt
1/8 teaspoon pepper
1 (6-ounce) can tuna, drained
1 cup shredded Monterey Jack cheese

Cook mushrooms in butter until soft. Combine soup, sour cream, mayonnaise, evaporated milk, salt and pepper. Mix until smooth. Add mushrooms, tuna and cheese. Place in freezer bag. Label and freeze. 6 servings.

To serve: Thaw. Heat and stir until smooth and bubbly and cheese is melted. Serve over hot buttered noodles.

 For **Chicken Stroganoff**, substitute 1 cup cooked, chopped chicken for the tuna.

Tuna Chow Mein

1 (10.75-ounce) can cream of mushroom soup
1 cup milk
2 tablespoons soy sauce
1 teaspoon sugar
1 (6-ounce) can tuna, drained
1 cup sliced celery
1 (8-ounce) can sliced water chestnuts, drained
1 cup chunked onion
1 (4-ounce) can sliced mushrooms, drained
1 (12-ounce) bag chow mein noodles

Combine soup, milk, soy sauce and sugar. Mix well. Stir in tuna, celery, water chestnuts, onion and mushrooms. (Do not add chow mein noodles until baking.) Place in freezer bag. Label and freeze. 6 servings.

To serve: Thaw. Pour into greased baking dish. Bake covered for 45 minutes at 350°. Uncover and top with half of the chow mein noodles. Bake 10 additional minutes. Serve with hot rice and remaining chow mein noodles.

 For **Chicken Chow Mein**, substitute 1 cup cooked, chopped chicken for the tuna.

Tuna Broccoli AuGratin

3 cups uncooked wide noodles
1 (10.75-ounce) can Cheddar cheese soup
3/4 cup evaporated milk
2 (6-ounce) cans tuna, drained
1/4 cup minced onion
1 (10-ounce) frozen broccoli
1 cup shredded American cheese

Cook noodles in boiling, salted water for 2 minutes less than shortest time recommended on package. Combine soup and milk. Mix until smooth. Add drained tuna and onion. Thaw and squeeze water from broccoli. Add to tuna mixture. Stir in cheese. Place in freezer bag. Label and freeze. 8 servings.

To serve: Thaw. Pour into greased baking dish. Bake covered for 45 minutes at 350°. Uncover. Top with more shredded cheese and bake an additional 5 minutes or until the cheese is melted.

 If the American cheese is too difficult to shred, cut or tear the cheese into small strips or pieces so it can be evenly distributed throughout the recipe. Substitute Cheddar cheese, if desired.

For **Chicken Broccoli AuGratin**, substitute 2 cups cooked, chopped chicken for the tuna.

Recipe Index

Almost Ravioli, 160
Bacon
  Bacon Chicken, 108
  Bacon Meatloaf, 176
  Calico Beans, 107
  Continental Chicken, 89
  Corn Chowder, 136
  Mock Filet Mignon, 195
Baked Chicken in Gravy, 110
Barbeque
  Barbeque Beef and Biscuits, 170
  Country Barbequed Ribs, 85
  Country Style Barbeque Ribs, 101
  Honey Barbequed Ribs, 71
  Skillet Barbeque Chicken, 153
  Skillet Barbeque Pork Chops, 149
  Slow Cooked Short Ribs, 77
Basic Meatballs, 183
Beans
  Biscuit Beef Bake, 169
  Cabbage Patch Stew, 130
  Calico Beans, 107
  Chili, 124
  Chili Soup, 125
  Cowboy Barbeque, 171
  Minestrone, 98
  New England Baked Beans, 93
  Old Fashioned Bean Soup, 94
  Slow Cooked Chili, 97
  Southwest Stew, 131
  Taco Soup, 132
Beef *(see also Beef, Ground)*
  Beef and Cheese Roll-Ups, 189
  Beef and Pork Chop Suey, 129
  Beef Stroganoff, 80
  Chicken Fried Steak, 151
  Corned Beef and Cabbage, 82
  Grandma's Beef Stew, 79
  Italian Roast, 83
  Maple Almond Beef, 140
  Mexican Beef Stew, 133
  Minestrone, 98
  Oven Stew, 102
  Slow Cooked Goulash, 78

Beef (continued)
  Slow Cooked Short Ribs, 77
  Slow Cooked Stew, 76
  Slow Cooked Stroganoff, 76
  Smothered Steak, 84
  Steak and Vegetable Pie, 191
  Swiss Steak and Gravy, 73
  Teriyaki Beef, 137
  Tomato Beef Stew, 103
  Tomato Swiss Steak, 74
  Vegetable Beef Soup, 96
Beef, Ground
  Almost Ravioli, 160
  Bacon Meat Loaf, 176
  Basic Meatballs, 183
  Barbeque Beef and Biscuits, 170
  Beef and Broccoli, 192
  Beef Noodle Onion Bake, 168
  Beef Stuffing Bake, 159
  Beefy Chinese Rice, 188
  Beefy Macaroni, 167
  Beefy Spanish Rice, 128
  Bird's Nest Pie, 157
  Biscuit Beef Bake, 169
  Cabbage Patch Stew, 130
  Calico Beans, 107
  California Dip Meat Loaf, 180
  Cantonese Meatballs, 123
  Cheesy Lasagna, 186
  Cheesy Meat Loaf,174
  Chili, 124
  Chili Beef and Rice, 190
  Chili Soup, 125
  Corny Meat Loaf, 179
  Cowboy Barbeque, 171
  Creamed Corn and Beef, 166
  Glazed Meat Loaf, 177
  Ground Beef Stroganoff, 194
  Hawaiian Meatballs, 142
  Italian Chili, 134
  Italian Meat Sauce, 95
  Italian Shells, 165
  Jack Soup, 126
  Lasagna, 121

Beef, Ground (continued)
Meatball Soup, 138
Meatball Spaghetti, 122
Meatballs in Gravy, 106
Meatballs in Sour Cream Sauce, 184
Meat Loaf and Potatoes, 172
Mexican Lasagna, 187
Mock Filet Mignon, 195
Nacho Meat Loaf, 178
Onion Soup Meat Loaf, 175
Pineapple Meatballs, 105
Pizza in a Dish, 193
Pizza Meat Loaf, 173
Porcupine Meatballs, 104
Ravioli Soup, 120
Salisbury Steak and Gravy, 139
Simply Lasagna, 164
Slow Cooked Chili, 97
Southwest Stew, 131
Spaghetti and Company, 161
Spaghetti and Meatballs, 185
Spaghetti Sauce, 119
Stuffing Meat Loaves, 182
Swedish Meatballs, 81
Sweet and Sour Meatballs, 141
Taco Pie, 158
Taco Soup, 132
Tomato Stroganoff, 127
Very Best Meat Loaf, 181
Bird's Nest Pie, 157
Biscuit Beef Bake, 169
Broccoli Chicken and Rice, 199
Brown Sugar Pork Ribs, 72
Cabbage Patch Stew, 130
Calico Beans, 107
California Dip Meat Loaf, 180
Candied Chicken, 111
Cantonese Meatballs, 123
Cheese Manicotti, 162
Cheesy Chicken and Rice, 202
Cheesy Ham and Noodles, 220
Cheesy Ham and Potatoes, 217
Cheesy Lasagna, 186
Cheesy Meat Loaf, 174

Chicken
Bacon Chicken, 108
Baked Chicken in Gravy, 110
Broccoli Chicken and Rice, 199
Candied Chicken, 111
Cheesy Chicken and Rice, 202
Chicken à la King, 145
Chicken and Biscuits, 203
Chicken and Broccoli, 198
Chicken and Dressing, 201
Chicken and Ham Dinner, 211
Chicken and Mushrooms, 147
Chicken and Rice, 204
Chicken Cacciatore, 88
Chicken Cordon Bleu, 117
Chicken Enchiladas, 209
Chicken Ham Roll-Ups, 148
Chicken Stroganoff, 146
Chicken Stuffed Manicotti, 163
Chicken Tortellini Soup, 135
Chicken with Mushroom Gravy, 87
Cola Chicken, 150
Continental Chicken, 89
Corkscrew Chicken, 196
Cornflake Chicken, 116
Country Chicken and Vegetables, 207
Cranberry Chicken, 112
Cream Cheese Chicken, 86
Creamy Chicken and Pasta, 212
Green Chile Chicken Soup, 200
Ham and Chicken Roll-Ups, 210
Hawaiian Chicken, 113
Honey Lime Chicken, 143
Mayonnaise Chicken, 206
Navajo Tacos, 197
Peachy Chicken, 109
Skillet Barbeque Chicken, 153
Smoky Maple Chicken, 115
Sweet and Sour Chicken, 144
Teriyaki Chicken, 114
Tortilla Chicken, 208
Chicken Fried Steak, 151
Chili
Chili, 124

Chili (continued)
  Chili Beef and Rice, 190
  Chili Soup, 125
  Italian Chili, 134
  Slow Cooked Chili, 97
Cola Chicken, 150
Continental Chicken, 89
Corkscrew Chicken, 196
Corn Chowder, 136
Corned Beef and Cabbage, 82
Cornflake Chicken, 116
Corny Meat Loaf, 179
Country Barbequed Ribs, 85
Country Chicken and Vegetables, 207
Country Style Barbeque Ribs, 101
Cowboy Barbeque, 171
Crab, Shrimp or Lobster Newberg, 90
Cranberry Chicken, 112
Cream Cheese Chicken, 86
Creamed Corn and Beef, 166
Creamy Chicken and Pasta, 212
French Onion Soup, 99
Glazed Meat Loaf, 177
Grandma's Beef Stew, 79
Green Chile Chicken Soup, 198
Ground Beef Stroganoff, 194
Ham
  Cheesy Ham and Noodles, 220
  Cheesy Ham and Potatoes, 217
  Chicken and Ham Dinner, 211
  Chicken Ham Roll-Ups, 148
  Ham and Chicken Roll-Ups, 210
  Ham and Noodles, 216
  Ham and Potato Scallop, 218
  Ham Loaf with Pineapple Sauce, 214
  Ham Primavera, 221
  New England Baked Beans, 93
  Old Fashioned Bean Soup, 94
  Swiss Ham and Noodles, 219
Hawaiian Chicken, 113
Hawaiian Meatballs, 142
Honey Barbequed Ribs, 71
Honey Lime Chicken, 143

Italian Chili, 134
Italian Meat Sauce, 95
Italian Roast, 83
Italian Shells, 165
Jack Soup, 126
Lasagna, 121
Manhattan Clam Chowder, 92
Maple Almond Beef, 140
Mayonnaise Chicken, 206
Meatballs
  Basic Meatballs, 183
  Cantonese Meatballs, 123
  Hawaiian Meatballs, 142
  Meatball Soup, 138
  Meatball Spaghetti, 122
  Meatballs in Gravy, 106
  Meatballs in Sour Cream Sauce, 184
  Pineapple Meatballs, 105
  Porcupine Meatballs, 104
  Spaghetti and Meatballs, 185
  Swedish Meatballs, 81
  Sweet and Sour Meatballs, 141
Meat Loaf
  Bacon Meat Loaf, 176
  California Dip Meat Loaf, 180
  Cheesy Meat Loaf, 174
  Corny Meat Loaf, 179
  Glazed Meat Loaf, 177
  Ham Loaf with Pineapple Sauce, 214
  Meat Loaf and Potatoes, 172
  Nacho Meat Loaf, 178
  Onion Soup Meat Loaf, 175
  Pizza Meat Loaf, 173
  Pork Loaf with Applesauce Glaze, 215
  Stuffing Meat Loaves, 182
  Very Best Meat Loaf, 181
Mexican Beef Stew, 133
Mexican Lasagna, 187
Minestrone, 98
Mock Filet Mignon, 195
Nacho Meat Loaf, 178
Navajo Tacos, 197
New England Baked Beans, 93

New England Clam Chowder, 91
Old Fashioned Bean Soup, 94
Onion Soup Meat Loaf, 175
Oven Stew, 102
Pasta
  Almost Ravioli, 160
  Beef Noodle Onion Bake, 168
  Beefy Macaroni, 167
  Bird's Nest Pie, 157
  Cheese Manicotti, 162
  Cheesy Ham and Noodles, 220
  Cheesy Lasagna, 186
  Chicken Stuffed Manicotti, 163
  Chicken Tortellini Soup, 135
  Corkscrew Chicken, 196
  Creamed Corn and Beef, 166
  Creamy Chicken and Pasta, 212
  Ham and Noodles, 216
  Ham Primavera, 221
  Italian Shells, 165
  Lasagna, 121
  Meatball Spaghetti, 122
  Mexican Lasagna, 187
  Minestrone, 98
  Pizza in a Dish, 193
  Ravioli Soup, 120
  Simply Lasagna, 164
  Spaghetti and Company, 161
  Spaghetti and Meatballs, 185
  Spaghetti Sauce, 119
  Swiss Ham and Noodles, 219
  Tuna Bow Ties, 224
  Tuna Broccoli AuGratin, 228
  Tuna Fettuccine, 225
Peachy Chicken, 109
Pineapple Meatballs, 105
Pizza in a Dish, 193
Pizza Meat Loaf, 173
Polynesian Pork Roast, 75
Porcupine Meatballs, 104
Pork *(See also Ham, Ribs)*
  Beef and Pork Chop Suey, 129
  Brown Sugar Pork Ribs, 72

Pork (continued)
  Country Barbequed Ribs, 85
  Country Style Barbeque Ribs, 101
  Honey Barbequed Ribs, 71
  Polynesian Pork Roast, 75
  Pork Chops and Potatoes, 222
  Pork Chops, Carrots & Gravy, 154
  Pork Loaf with Applesauce Glaze, 215
  Scalloped Pork Chops, 223
  Skillet Barbeque Pork Chops, 149
Ravioli Soup, 120
Ribs
  Brown Sugar Pork Ribs, 72
  Country Barbequed Ribs, 85
  Country Style Barbeque Ribs, 101
  Honey Barbequed Ribs, 71
  Slow Cooked Short Ribs, 77
Rice
  Beef and Broccoli, 192
  Beefy Chinese Rice, 188
  Beefy Spanish Rice, 128
  Broccoli Chicken and Rice, 199
  Cheesy Chicken and Rice, 202
  Chicken and Rice, 204
  Chili Beef and Rice, 190
  Ham and Chicken Roll-Ups, 210
  Mayonnaise Chicken, 206
Salisbury Steak and Gravy, 139
Scalloped Pork Chops, 223
Seafood *(See also Tuna)*
  Crab, Shrimp or Lobster Newberg, 90
  Manhattan Clam Chowder, 92
  New England Clam Chowder, 91
Simply Lasagna, 164
Skillet Barbeque Chicken, 153
Skillet Barbeque Pork Chops, 149
Slow Cooked Chili, 97
Slow Cooked Goulash, 78
Slow Cooked Short Ribs, 77
Slow Cooked Stew, 76
Slow Cooked Stroganoff, 76
Smoky Maple Chicken, 115
Smothered Steak, 84

Soup
  Chicken Tortellini Soup, 135
  Chili Soup, 125
  Corn Chowder, 136
  French Onion Soup, 99
  Green Chile Chicken Soup, 200
  Jack Soup, 126
  Manhattan Clam Chowder, 92
  Meatball Soup, 138
  Minestrone, 98
  New England Clam Chowder, 91
  Old Fashioned Bean Soup, 94
  Ravioli Soup, 120
  Taco Soup, 132
  Vegetable Beef Soup, 96
Southwest Stew, 131
Spaghetti and Company, 161
Spaghetti and Meatballs, 185
Spaghetti Sauce, 119
Steak and Vegetable Pie, 191
Stew
  Cabbage Patch Stew, 130
  Grandma's Beef Stew, 79
  Mexican Beef Stew, 133
  Oven Stew, 102
  Slow Cooked Stew, 76
  Southwest Stew, 131
  Tomato Beef Stew, 103
Stuffing
  Beef Stuffing Bake, 159
  Chicken and Dressing, 201
  Stuffing Meat Loaves, 182
  Turkey and Stuffing Roll-Ups, 213
  Turkey Dressing Pie, 205
Swedish Meatballs, 81
Sweet and Sour Chicken, 144
Sweet and Sour Meatballs, 141
Swiss Ham and Noodles, 219
Swiss Steak and Gravy, 73
Taco Pie, 158
Taco Soup, 132
Teriyaki Beef, 137
Teriyaki Chicken, 114
Tomato Beef Stew, 103
Tomato Stroganoff, 127

Tomato Swiss Steak, 74
Tortilla Chicken, 208
Tuna
  Tuna Bow Ties, 224
  Tuna Broccoli AuGratin, 228
  Tuna Chow Mein, 227
  Tuna Fettuccine, 225
  Tuna Stroganoff, 226
Turkey
  Turkey and Stuffing Roll-Ups, 213
  Turkey Dressing Pie, 205
  Waikiki Turkey, 152
Vegetable Beef Soup, 96
Very Best Meat Loaf, 181
Waikiki Turkey, 152